Write from the Heart

POETRY PLAYGROUND

Poetry Curriculum for All Writers

By Veldorah J. Rice

TEACHER'S MANUAL
Lesson Plans, Guided Activities, & Grading Options

Poetry Playground: Teacher's Manual by Veldorah J. Rice
Published by Write from the Heart
PO Box 1451
Indiana, Pa 15701
www.WriteFromTheHeart.org

Copyright © 2025 Veldorah J. Rice

All rights reserved. No portion of this book may be reproduced in any form without permission from the publisher, except as permitted by U.S. copyright law. For permissions contact: inquiry@writefromtheheart.org

For information about special discounts available for bulk purchases, sales promotions, fund-raising and educational needs, contact Write from the Heart at inquiry@writefromtheheart.org.

All student examples used by permission.

Printed in the United States of America

First Edition

ISBN: 978-1-954272-46-0 (paperback)

ISBN: 978-1-954272-47-7 (ebook)

Welcome to Poetry Playground

Poetry is an amazing way to express how YOU see the world. This course helps you use your thoughts, feelings, and experiences to create poetry that is expressive and fun.

Each lesson, you'll step into the world of words, sounds, and structures. You'll explore poetic tools that help you experiment with voice, rhythm, and imagery, techniques that transform your thoughts into art. Guided by professional poets and student examples, you'll experiment with different poetry styles, discovering how your choices create unique effects.

There are no length requirements on any pieces of creative writing for a reason: you are welcome to make your poems as long or as short as you would like! Some assignments have parameters to tell you what must be included, but you are the one who gets to choose if your poems rhyme (or not), how many stanzas you need, and what words you use. This is your space to take risks and be creative.

You don't have to be perfect to get started. The goal isn't perfection—it's progress. By the end of this course, you'll have a stronger voice, a deeper understanding of how poetry works, and a toolkit of strategies you can use anytime you write—in school or just for yourself.

About Write from the Heart

Write from the Heart is a writing and literature program designed to nurture students as thinkers, communicators, and creators. With a focus on voice, structure, and expression, we help students build confidence in their writing while engaging deeply with the writing process. Our courses emphasize authenticity, creativity, and critical thinking—equipping students not just to meet academic goals, but to communicate meaningfully in the world around them. We support students from middle school through high school, with a special focus on college preparation and a unique AP English class. We also provide tracks for students going to technical schools or the workforce, with a focus on practical and business writing.

Write from the Heart is built on the belief that writing should be both purposeful and personal. Whether students are crafting analytical essays, personal narratives, or imaginative stories, our curriculum helps them find their voice and strengthen their skills. We support students and families through flexible, engaging courses that are rooted in interactive instruction. Students receive individualized instruction in a collaborative environment.

Write from the Heart offers a wide range of writing programs to meet different needs and learning styles. Our full-credit annual classes include daily instructor support, while our semester-based courses offer weekly instructor interaction for half-credit. We also provide workshops in special topics, private coaching for individualized support, and a growing collection of books, workbooks, and journals. For families and schools seeking flexibility, our self-paced curriculum includes both student and teacher manuals for independent learning.

Learn more at www.writefromtheheart.org

Welcome to the Teacher's Manual for Poetry Playground

Poetry gives students the rare opportunity to express themselves honestly, creatively, and powerfully. In a world where students are often told to write in structured, academic ways, poetry offers a space to explore voice, emotion, and perspective. This course was designed to help students find out new ways to express themselves on the page. Whether they are first-time poets or experienced writers, students will discover tools they can use to shape thoughts into images, emotions into language, and personal moments into powerful writing. Each unit breaks poetry down into manageable, focused lessons—making poetic techniques accessible, meaningful, and fun. Along the way, students become stronger writers overall: more intentional with word choice, more attuned to rhythm and structure, and more confident in their ability to revise.

The teacher's manual provides instructional support for each lesson, including clear objectives, overviews, content review connections, and teaching notes that highlight discussion points and suggested strategies. You'll find that each unit builds logically on the last, helping students deepen their understanding of poetry as they go.

This curriculum is especially effective when taught as a process. Students are encouraged to revise, reflect, and improve—not just to complete tasks. As you guide your students through these lessons, feel free to adapt pacing, model responses, and add your own examples to meet the needs of your classroom. Writing is a personal process, and this course provides the structure to support each student's individual growth within that process.

Poetry is personal, and so is the learning process. This curriculum encourages creative risk-taking, flexibility, and voice. You'll find that many assignments are open-ended—on purpose. There are no length requirements, no "right" answers, and no required rhyme. Your role is to help students explore poetic tools, develop their unique voices, and revise their work with increasing confidence.

Each unit includes:

- **An overview of the unit focus**, so you can frame the big picture
- **Teaching tips** for introducing concepts and helping students engage
- **Sample student responses** to model techniques and spark discussion
- **Extension and modification ideas** to challenge advanced writers or support struggling ones

You don't need to be a poetry expert to use this course. The lessons do the heavy lifting—you provide the encouragement, structure, and space for your students to grow. As they experiment with word choice, line breaks, imagery, and more, you'll watch their voices emerge with clarity and confidence. And you are certainly welcome to join in and complete the lessons yourself!

We recommend focusing on the process of growth rather than meeting the elements of a rubric. Encourage students to share their work aloud when possible, and remind them that revision is part of the creative process—not a sign that they've done something wrong. We do provide methods for grading, but also include credit for self-evaluation and revision. You are also welcome to simply enjoy the process with your students and look for benchmarks of understanding–we provide the materials to grade that way as well.

Above all, this course is designed to be playful, personal, and expressive. Let students make bold choices. Let them write badly before they write better. Celebrate the process as much as the product.

Suggested Course Pacing and Scoring Options

The *Poetry Playground* curriculum is designed to be flexible and adaptable. Below are three pacing models to help you plan how to deliver the material in your classroom or homeschool setting. Each option is based on your available time, instructional goals, and the needs of your students.

> **Option 1: 5-6-Week Intensive (One Unit per Week)**
> *Ideal for a standard quarter-length course or short-term writing bootcamp.*
>
> - **Weekly Schedule:**
>   - **Monday:** Lesson 1 (instruction + start activities)
>   - **Tuesday & Wednesday:** Complete Lesson 1 activities
>   - **Thursday:** Lesson 2 (instruction + share with peers option)
>   - **Friday:** Complete Lesson 2 activities
>
> **Notes:**
>   - This option works well when students already have some writing experience.
>   - Complete the "Bonus Review" as either an activity in Week 5 or complete it as the final wrap-up in Week 6. Use one day for Step 1 and two days each for Steps 2 & 3.

Option 2: 10-Week Standard (1 Lesson per Week)
Best for semester or quarter-long enrichment classes, co-ops, or focused writing instruction.
- **Weekly Schedule:**
  - **Day 1:** Introduce the lesson with instruction, discussion, and examples
  - **Days 2–4:** Students complete activities independently or in class
  - **Day 5:** Peer discussion or teacher feedback

Notes:
  - This pacing keeps students focused on one skill at a time.
  - This is designed for students to write or revise one poem per day on days 2-4.

Option 3: 12–15 Week Relaxed Pace (Split Lessons)
Best for semester courses or low-pressure settings or students who need extra time.
- **Weekly Schedule:**
  - **Week 1:** Introduce the first half of the lesson (concept and examples); include in-depth discussion of examples
  - **Week 2:** Complete activities and reflect on learning
  - **Repeat weekly for each lesson**

  Notes:
  - This allows for deeper discussion and slower scaffolding of skills.
  - You may choose to assign peer interactions in between each activity in Week 2
  - The "Bonus Revision Lesson" could be taught on this two-week schedule as well, using one week for revisions and the second week for writing and conferencing new poems.

Scoring Options:

Poetry is a difficult genre of writing to grade. It is extremely personal and intimate, and attaching a grade can be hard for both teachers and students. At the same time, we want to be able to help students see their growth, and teachers often want to know how to assign points for the work.

However, this curriculum isn't about making the "right" kind of poem, and we know that the difference between a "good" and "bad" poem is often a matter of taste. So throughout the class we offer three ways to grade.

Traditional Grading: this track offers rubrics and measurable markers of learning. Rubrics are provided in Appendix A and scoring reminders are included in each activity, with a gradebook in Appendix B.

Benchmark Grading: this track offers "completion markers" to look for in each assignment–they get full points if they attempt each portion of the activity appropriately. Scoring suggestions are listed in each activity, with a gradebook in Appendix B.

Pass/Fail Grading: this track should include a simple pass/fail marker for completing the activity. Note: this track is not noted in each activity, but a gradebook for this method is included in Appendix B to record completions.

Regardless of how you grade, it is not unusual for poems to get full credit and for students to have perfect or near-perfect scores in a class like this. We are not looking for errors the way we would in a traditional essay. Here, we are looking to reward and celebrate creativity!

Final Tip:

Regardless of your pacing, keep time open for revision and reflection. Students benefit most when they're given space to create.

Table of Contents

UNIT 1: THE TOOLS OF POETRY 19

Lesson 1: Introduction to Poetry 20

Lesson 1 Activity A 24

Lesson 1 Activity B 28

Lesson 1 Activity C 31

Lesson 2: Revising Poetry 38

Lesson 2 Activity 42

UNIT 2: STRUCTURING POETRY 44

Lesson 3: Lines & Stanzas 45

Lesson 3 Activity A 54

Lesson 3 Activity B 58

Lesson 3 Activity C 61

Lesson 4: Revising Poetry Structures 65

Lesson 4 Activity 70

UNIT 3: SOUND QUALITY 72

Lesson 5: Sound Quality 73

Lesson 5 Activity A 81

Lesson 5 Activity B 83

Lesson 5 Activity C 86

Lesson 6: Revising Poetry Sound Quality 91

Lesson 6 Activity 96

UNIT 4: WORD CHOICE 99

Lesson 7: Word Choice 100

Lesson 7 Activity A 110

Lesson 7 Activity B 113

Lesson 7 Activity C 115

Lesson 8: Revising Poetry 118

Lesson 8 Activity 122

UNIT 5: IMAGERY 124

Lesson 9: Imagery 125

Lesson 9 Activity A 136

Lesson 9 Activity B 140

Lesson 9 Activity C 142

Lesson 10: Revising Poetry Imagery 146

Lesson 10 Activity 149

BONUS REVISION LESSON: Final Poetry Activity 151

APPENDIX A: SCORING RUBRICS 155

APPENDIX B: GRADE TRACKING 159

Student Course Overview

Unit 1: The Tools of Poetry

Lesson 1

- ☐ Read "Introduction to Poetry"

This lesson gives an overview of the four main tools we will explore in the course: structure, sound quality, word choice, and imagery, and we will start writing poems!

Activity:

- ☐ Complete the "Kitchen Poem" Activity
- ☐ Complete the "Picture-Object Poem" Activity
- ☐ Complete the "Persona Confession Poem" Activity

Lesson 2

- ☐ Read "Revising Poetry–What's the Heart of the Poem?"

In this lesson, we will discuss revising poetry and how to make your original poems better!

Activity:

- ☐ Complete the "Revising Lesson 1's Poems" activity.

Unit 2: Structuring Poetry

Lesson 3

- ☐ Read "Lines & Stanzas"

Why does poetry look so weird? How do I know when to go to the next line? Should I capitalize or punctuate certain words? How do I know the rules? All your burning questions are answered in this lesson!

Activity:

- ☐ Complete the "Line Break Poem" Activity
- ☐ Complete the "One-Sentence Poem" Activity
- ☐ Complete the "Line-Builder Poem" Activity

Lesson 4

- ☐ Read "Revising Poetry Structures"

In this lesson, we will further discuss revising poetry around structures and line breaks.

Activity:

- ☐ Complete the "Revising Lesson 3's Poems" activity.

Unit 3: Sound Quality

Lesson 5

☐ Read "Sound Quality"

This lesson focuses on sound: the way words sound, and how to use that to create rhythm and meter in poetry. We will practice with sound poems.

Activity:

☐ Complete the "Random Words, Deliberate Sounds Poem" Activity
☐ Complete the "Nonsense Poem" Activity
☐ Complete the "Popping Popcorn Poem" Activity

Lesson 6

☐ Read "Revising Poetry Sound Quality"

In this lesson, we will focus on revising the sounds of your poetry.

Activity:

☐ Complete the "Revising Lesson 5's Poems" activity.

Unit 4: Word Choice

Lesson 7

☐ Read "Word Choice"

This lesson looks at words and how slightly different words can create slightly different meanings. We will play with words with our poems!

Activity:

☐ Complete the "Line-by-Line Poem" Activity
☐ Complete the "Nouns & Verbs Poem" Activity
☐ Complete the "Tone Shift Poem" Activity

Lesson 8

☐ Read "Revising Poetry"

In this lesson, we will discuss revising poetry and how to make your
original poems better!

Activity:

☐ Complete the "Revising Lesson 7's Poems" activity.

Unit 5: Imagery

Lesson 9

- ☐ Read "Imagery"

This lesson looks at the way we create pictures with our words: from descriptive language to personification to metaphors, we cover it all and try it all!

Activity:

- ☐ Complete the "Afterimages Poem" Activity
- ☐ Complete the "Postcard Poem" Activity
- ☐ Complete the "What the Object Knows Poem" Activity

Lesson 10

- ☐ Read "Revising Poetry Imagery"

In this lesson, we will look at revising the images in poetry and how to make your original poems better! We will also have a final round-up of all your poetry from this course.

Activity:

- ☐ Complete the "Revising Lesson 9's Poems" activity.

Bonus Revision Lesson: Final Poetry Activity

UNIT 1:
THE TOOLS OF POETRY

In this unit, you'll take your first steps into the world of poetry. You'll learn what makes a poem different from other writing and experiment with using your own voice in new and creative ways. You'll also explore how to take a first-try poem and shape it into something stronger through revision. These lessons are designed to show you that poetry isn't about "getting it right"—it's about expressing yourself, playing with language, and discovering the tools that poets use to bring their ideas to life.

Unit Objective:

Students will be able to identify and experiment with the basic building blocks of poetry—including structure, word choice, sound quality, and imagery—and begin to use these tools intentionally to shape their own writing.

Unit Overview:

This first unit introduces students to the idea that poetry is more than just rhyming lines or feelings on paper—it's crafted, deliberate, and full of choices. Students will explore how poets use tools like theme, word choice, and structure to express something deeper. They'll see how these tools shape meaning and voice, and begin to experiment with them in their own work. Because this is the opening unit, the goal is exposure and exploration—not mastery. This unit sets the tone for the course: poetry as a creative process that blends intention with imagination.

Each lesson includes opportunities to share, reflect, and revise. While the writing tasks are short, they are designed to invite deep thinking and spark creativity. Encourage students to take their time with word choice and structure—even if the poem is brief. Let them explore what their voice sounds like when they have full creative control.

Lesson 1: Introduction to Poetry

Objective:
Students will identify and experiment with foundational poetic tools and apply at least one of these tools in an original poem.

Overview:
This lesson introduces students to the idea that poetry is a crafted form of writing, full of deliberate choices. Rather than relying on feelings alone, strong poetry uses tools—like word choice, sound quality, imagery, and structure—to express meaning in a powerful way. Students will explore an overview of these tools through short examples and guided activities before drafting a poem of their own. The emphasis in this lesson is creative exploration and voice: students are not expected to use (or even fully understand) every tool, but they should begin to see how each technique changes a poem's effect. This sets the foundation for deeper analysis and revision in future units.

Teaching Notes:
- **Start with the idea of poetry as a toolbox.** Many students enter poetry either intimidated by it or overly casual about it. Framing the tools as creative options (not rules) helps open their thinking.
- **Encourage experimentation.** Some students will naturally gravitate toward a specific style or structure, while others may struggle with them. Remind students that the goal is to *try* each activity, not to perfect it.
- **Use the examples for discussion, not just modeling.** Read the student and professional poems aloud and ask students what they notice. Which lines stand out? Which tools are being used? Which ones feel more effective or emotional?
- **Let students play.** These activities are meant to help them

explore different techniques before committing to a final poem. The emphasis should be on using that tool with purpose and voice.
- **Optional share session.** If your environment allows, consider having students read their final poems aloud or share them in pairs. This builds confidence early in the course and reminds them that poetry is a form of communication—not just a private exercise.

Poetry is a daunting genre to many people. They find the format difficult and often feel like they don't know what a poem is "saying" because of the specialized way in which it is written. In order to feel more comfortable reading and writing poetry, a good place to start is to talk about the elements that make up a poem.

The poem is a special kind of writing. Writing a poem is using language and writing structure in a unique way to express a writer's view of the world. There is not a strict set of rules for writing poetically. A poem can rhyme, or not. It can be short, like a haiku, or a book-length epic. It can break all the rules or stick to a strict structure.

However, poets, just like other artists, have their own set of "tools" to use. A sculptor might make an abstract piece or the statue of David, but he still uses the same thing: a hammer and chisel. Maybe one sculptor uses very small tools, and another one works in large, rough style. Poetry works that way, too. Every writer is different, and so is their poetic styling. We all work out of the same toolbox, but the tools we choose to utilize might be different from another poet's.

We will be talking about each of these things in more depth throughout the class, but here are the general tools that a poet has at his or her disposal:
- **Structure**—the way a poem is set up as whole. Does it rhyme? Have three stanzas of four lines each? Do the lines

break in strange places? We will talk about how structure can change the meaning of your poem. We will be looking at this in Unit 2.

- **Sound Quality**—how a poet uses language. This might be rhyming words or matching the first consonants of words in a line. This can also be using onomatopoeia. Language has a sound, even when it is read on the page. We will be focusing on this in Unit 3.
- **Word Choice**—what words a poet uses. Porridge is different from cereal. Robin is different from bird. Woman is different from girl. Picking the right verbs, adjectives, adverbs, and nouns can make all the difference in a poem. This is the focus of Unit 4.
- **Imagery**—the way a poet creates an emotion or experience within a poem. Explaining an abstract term in concrete language is difficult. I can tell you that I have a green two-wheeler bike with a frayed banana seat, but how do I tell you what it feels like to ride it down the biggest hill in my town? Creating a picture with words or using similes and metaphors are some of the ways a poet can do this. We will be looking at this in Unit 5.

All these tools work together to create a poem. Writing poetry is one of the most personal forms of writing and is often described as a "concentrated" form of writing. Every single word matters, and there is often more than one way to understand a line.

For example, take this poem by Percy Shelly, written in 1821.

> The flower that smiles to-day
> To-morrow dies;
> All that we wish to stay
> Tempts and then flies.
> What is this world's delight?

Lightning that mocks the night,
Brief even as bright.

On the surface, this poem seems to be about flowers and nature. But what if we think about these items as being metaphors for something else? What if we replace "flower" with "human"? Well, now the poem is maybe about how quickly life goes by, and how something could happen to cut life short—"Lightning" could be an accident, or an illness or anything else like that.

Poets do this all the time. Nature is often a stand-in for our humanity. Here are a few more examples:

Ah Sun-flower! weary of time,
Who countest the steps of the Sun:
Seeking after that sweet golden clime
Where the travellers journey is done.
—William Blake

As for man, his days are like grass;
 he flourishes like a flower of the field;
for the wind passes over it, and it is gone,
 and its place knows it no more.
—Psalms of David

You can see here how each of these poems used the same metaphor (flower=human life) but they used different words and structures to show their thoughts. Some of them rhyme, and some don't. Some play with punctuation and capitalization, while others follow conventional rules. Poetry gives you the freedom to express yourself with many different options.

Lesson 1 Activity A: Kitchen Poem

Purpose of the Activity:
This activity helps students understand how poetry can come from everyday life and objects—no dramatic events required. By setting a poem in a kitchen and using specific sensory details, students practice using concrete language, mood, and theme. The prompt also encourages students to think about space, tone, and emotional context, all while writing within a familiar setting. This is an excellent opportunity for students to explore imagery, contrast, and perspective.

Have the student complete the activity on their own, or use the guided learning together.

Guided Learning:
1. **Introduce the idea of "poetry in the ordinary.**
   Ask students to think about how many poems focus on small, everyday moments. A kitchen might not seem poetic—but it's full of sounds, smells, textures, routines, and memories. The goal is to look closer.
2. **Let the students color.**
   Encourage the students to draw a picture with crayons. After they finish, help them notice what colors they used and what objects they took the time to include. Those things make for great ideas for the poem!
3. **Brainstorm together.**
   Ask students to make a list of kitchen objects, sounds, smells, or memories. Prompt with questions like:
   - What does your kitchen smell like in the morning?
   - What's the loudest sound in a kitchen?
   - What's the most interesting object in a kitchen?
   - What memory does a certain dish or drawer hold?
4. **Review the example poem.**
   Have students read the example provided in the workbook.

Ask:
- What is the setting?
- Where do they see the author including the required elements of the poem?
- What is the mood or tone of each piece?
- How do the two poems differ? What is the same about them?

5. **Set writing expectations.**

    Students are asked to write a short poem that takes place in a kitchen. They can focus on a mood (cozy, chaotic, lonely, warm), a single object, or a memory. Review the elements that are required for the poem and ask how they will include it.

6. **Tie to Later Lessons:**

    Remind students that this is an introductory poem and they haven't learned all the tools yet! They will be given the opportunity to revise this poem both in the next lesson and at the end of the course.

Scoring Options:

Traditional Grading: Use the "Poem First Draft" Rubric found in Appendix A. Any poetic tool is acceptable for this activity. This poem is worth 20 points.

Benchmark Grading: This poem is worth 20 points. Award 8 points for completing the activity, and 3 points each for the four elements the student was required to include in the poem.

Directional Words

Write a poem about your mother's kitchen. Here are the rules:
- Using crayons, draw a picture of the kitchen (this really will help you—especially with description!).
- Use the picture to help you start the poem.
- Make sure the following things are in the poem:

- The oven
- Something green
- Something dead
- A female relation

You can use any form you would like—free verse, or a metered and rhymed poem. There is no length requirement.

Student Examples:

My Mother's Kitchen
By Gwen G, 16
    Crocodile green on the walls
    Light shining onto the floor
    The refrigerator is full of vegetables.
    But there's ice cream in the freezer down below.
    The room is under construction.
    It'll be a mess for a couple months.
    The oven will soon be gone.
    And so will the dishwasher.
    The flowers on the windowsill are dying.
    As my mom cooks soup for tonight.

Eggs or Salad
By Hattie C, 15
    The eggs are dancing on the stove,
    Assuring delightful sensation.
    Oh what a breakfast it will be,
    Satisfying and succulent.

    "Who wants lettuce?"
    Mom does ask,
    And in reply is heard:
    "Eggs for us, eggs for us, lettuce is just YUK."

    A fly was buzzing at the window,
    Just an hour ago.
    Buzzing to the hop-skip reel of eggs in the pan,

But now the fly is no more.

"Eggs for us, eggs for us, eggs are delicious."
Little do we suspect,
Oh we do notice,
The lettuce in our omelets.

Lesson 1 Activity B: Picture-Object Poem

Purpose of the Activity

This activity invites students to create a narrative poem inspired by a curated group of objects. Rather than focusing on one image, students are challenged to imagine a scene or character that connects all the items. This builds narrative thinking, encourages world-building, and pushes students to develop voice, mood, and structure within a poetic frame. It's also a chance to reinforce that poetry doesn't have to be abstract—it can tell a story.

Have the student complete the activity on their own, or use the guided learning together.

Guided Learning:

1. **Introduce the premise**

    Explain that poets sometimes begin with a question: *What does this group of things suggest?* In this case, students will use the provided images and imagine they are all found in the same room. The goal is to write a poem that captures a glimpse of a larger story—without needing to tell the full plot.

2. **Facilitate deep observation.**

    Ask students to look carefully at each item in the pictures. What are they made of? How are they arranged? Which one stands out most to them? Begin a brief class brainstorm about possible interpretations—just to get ideas flowing.

3. **Guide the story-thinking.**

    Have students answer brainstorming questions, either in writing or verbally:
    - Who owns these items?
    - What kind of room are they in?
    - What connects these objects?

- What event could have happened—or be about to happen—in this space?
- How would a stranger react if they walked in?
- What memories could it evoke if a relative walked in?

4. **Set the poetic challenge.**

   Go over the creative constraints:
   - The poem must mention *all* of the pictured objects.
   - Students can write in any voice (first-person, third-person, guest, owner, child, etc.).
   - The poem should be *story-based*—something should be happening, or have happened, in the space.
   - It's okay to leave parts of the story untold; the mystery is part of the poem's power.

5. **Encourage flexible structure.**

   Let students know their poem doesn't need to rhyme or follow a strict form. It can be fragmented, lyrical, or straightforward—what matters is that it captures a moment or mood in this imagined room.

Scoring Options:

Traditional Grading: Use the "Poem First Draft" Rubric found in Appendix A. Any poetic tool is acceptable for this activity. This poem is worth 20 points.

Benchmark Grading: This poem is worth 20 points. Award 8 points for completing the activity, and 3 points each for the four elements the student was required to include in the poem.

Look at the pictures below. Imagine they are all in the same room and create a story about the room and the owner(s) of these items. Think up more than what you might need in a poem. Who owns these items? Do they only have one owner? What is the room that they are in like? How did they all get there? What are they used for? How do(es) the owner(s) feel about the items, or the room they are in? If a stranger/guest entered the room, would the items be noticed, and why?

Brainstorm by making notes about the elements of the story of the room, or the owner, or the items, or anything you might like. It might help to create an incident or event that occurs in this room. The rules:

- You must mention all the objects in the poem.
- You can choose any speaker you like for the poem, or have it be in third person.
- You must write this as a story-poem. You do not need to tell us the whole story, though.

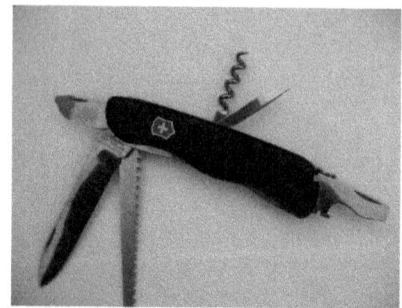

Lesson 1 Activity C: Persona Confession Poem

Purpose of the Activity:

This activity invites students to write from someone else's point of view—a persona poem that includes a "confession." It helps students practice voice, character development, tone, and perspective. By stepping into the mind of a real or imagined character (even an object or animal), students explore how language choices reveal identity and emotion. The addition of a confession helps deepen the emotional core of the poem while encouraging creative risk-taking and empathy.

Have the student complete the activity on their own, or use the guided learning together.

Guided Learning:

1. **Introduce the concept of persona poetry.**

   Let students know that a persona poem is written *in the voice* of someone else. That might be a real historical figure, a fictional character, or even an object with imagined thoughts. Use the phrase: "You are acting as this character—but with a pen."

2. **Review examples together.**

   Use the student and professional examples provided in the activity assignment, reading them carefully together. Highlight:
   - Vocabulary that reflects the character's voice or knowledge
   - The tone of the "confession" (serious, humorous, misunderstood, regretful, etc.)
   - How even simple lines give emotional depth (e.g., "I wasn't only ugly on the outside...")

3. **Brainstorm persona ideas.**

   Ask students to list possibilities:

- Characters from literature, fairy tales, or myth
- Historical or pop culture figures
- An imagined person with a specific occupation
- Animals or objects with human-like voices

If they need some help, guide them toward a person who has a contradiction: the typical "villain" of a story who is misunderstood; a historical figure with a fixed reputation that could be questioned (i.e. what if Abraham Lincoln told a lie when he was ten and still feels guilty about it?); or a nameless person with an occupation and a fear that are incongruent (i.e. a scuba diver who is terrified of fish)

4. **Choose a speaker and confession.**

   Once a persona is chosen, students should decide what the speaker will "confess." Encourage emotional variety—it could be funny, petty, profound, or surprising. The confession should help reveal something hidden or misunderstood.

5. **Create the voice.**

   Before writing, prompt students to think about:
   - How does this speaker talk? (word choice, sentence length, emotion)
   - What do they understand—or misunderstand—about their world?
   - Do they want to be forgiven, noticed, pitied, or admired? Or something else?

6. **Draft the poem.**

   Students write in first-person from the perspective of their chosen persona. It doesn't need to rhyme or follow a strict form. The most important thing is that it *sounds* like the speaker and contains a personal or emotional reveal. Usually the title includes the name of the person. The poem should include little details to connect the character to their story.

Scoring Options:
Traditional Grading: Use the "Poem First Draft" Rubric found in Appendix A. Any poetic tool is acceptable for this activity. This poem is worth 20 points.
Benchmark Grading: This poem is worth 20 points. Award 10 points for completing the activity, and 10 points for clearly creating a persona.

For this poem, you will not be writing in your own voice. Instead, you will be writing in the voice and with the "mind" of someone else. Here are the rules:
- Create a persona you will write as. This can be a real person, a person from fiction, a fairy tale, a story, or simply a made-up person from your imagination. It could also be an animal, or even an inanimate object.
- Make sure to give that person a "voice"—imagine how the persona would speak, and what vocabulary he/she/it would have.
- Have the persona "confess" something in the poem. It can be silly or serious.

Examples:

Knowlt Hoheimer
By Edgar Lee Masters

I was the first fruits of the battle of Missionary Ridge.
When I felt the bullet enter my heart
I wished I had staid at home and gone to jail
For stealing the hogs of Curl Trenary,
Instead of running away and joining the army.
Rather a thousand times the county jail
Than to lie under this marble figure with wings,

And this granite pedestal Bearing the words, "Pro Patria."
What do they mean, anyway?

(Note: the man—who is dead—is obviously uneducated...note the deliberate spelling error of "staid" instead of "stayed"!)

A Song in the Front Yard
By Gwendolyn Brooks

I've stayed in the front yard all my life.
I want a peek at the back
Where it's rough and untended and hungry weed grows.
A girl gets sick of a rose.

I want to go in the back yard now
And maybe down the alley,
To where the charity children play.
I want a good time today.
They do some wonderful things.
They have some wonderful fun.
My mother sneers, but I say it's fine
How they don't have to go in at quarter to nine.
My mother, she tells me that Johnnie Mae
Will grow up to be a bad woman.
That George'll be taken to Jail soon or late
(On account of last winter he sold our back gate).

But I say it's fine. Honest, I do.
And I'd like to be a bad woman, too,
And wear the brave stockings of night-black lace
And strut down the streets with paint on my face.

(Note: the little girl doesn't understand what a "bad woman" does—she just thinks it looks fun! This is an example of how you can play with a person's lack of knowledge)

Superman
By Five for Fighting (song)

I can't stand to fly
I'm not that naive
I'm just out to find
The better part of me

I'm more than a bird
I'm more than a plane
More than some pretty face beside a train
It's not easy to be me

Wish that I could cry
Fall upon my knees
Find a way to lie
About a home I'll never see

It may sound absurd but don't be naive
Even Heroes have the right to bleed
I may be disturbed but won't you concede
Even Heroes have the right to dream
It's not easy to be me

Up, up and away, away from me
It's all right
You can all sleep sound tonight
I'm not crazy, or anything

I can't stand to fly
I'm not that naive
Men weren't meant to ride
With clouds between their knees

I'm only a man in a silly red sheet
Digging for kryptonite on this one way street
Only a man in a funny red sheet
Looking for special things inside of me

It's not easy to be me.

Student Example

Cinderella's Step-Sister
By Christina B.

Cinderella pranced into my life when we were just kids
She always had it all – a father, beauty, a great voice
So it was only fair to take her money and freedom away, right?
Then her father died, but that wasn't my fault.

Even when she was a servant she made me feel so ugly
Her perfection added an exclamation mark to my flaws
Then she went and got the prince to fall in love with her
Now she's a queen, and I'm still the ugly step-sister

I guess it was all her fault, wasn't it?
She made me feel hideous
So she made me treat her badly, didn't she?
Yes – she forced me to!

Well, I didn't ask to be the ugly step-sister
That's the funny thing about life
People think they control everything
But they don't really have any power at all

I thought I controlled my beautiful step-sister
But I didn't, because at the end of the day
I wasn't only ugly on the outside
And she was always more than just good looking

See, I could have been beautiful on the inside
Like Cinderella, my perfect step-sister
But I guess everyone knows who I chose to be
Because I'm the ugly step-sister, inside and out

Lesson 2: Revising Poetry— What's the Heart of the Poem?

Objective:

Students will revise one or more of their poems with a focus on identifying and strengthening the central emotion, image, or message. They will evaluate their use of poetic tools and make deliberate changes that increase clarity, emotional impact, and poetic power.

Overview:

This revision lesson helps students take a step back from their drafts and evaluate what their poem is *really* saying. The focus is on clarity of message and intentional use of poetic tools. Rather than correcting or editing for perfection, students are encouraged to make meaningful choices: replacing a vague line with a stronger image, reworking a metaphor, or adjusting structure to sharpen meaning. The lesson also helps students see revision as a normal and essential part of writing—not as a punishment or fix for something "wrong." It's about refining, not repairing.

Content Review:

Before beginning this lesson, review the concept of poetic tools introduced in Lesson 1. Ask students to recall some of the techniques they explored—such as voice, structure, and mood—and how these tools helped shape the meaning or emotion of their poem. Emphasize that each tool is a *choice*, and that strong poems use those choices with purpose.

Teaching Notes:

- **Frame revision as growth, not correction.** Many students fear revising because they think it means their first draft "failed." Remind them that poets—like all writers—rework their lines constantly. Revision is where the real writing happens.
- **Use the sculpting metaphor.** Help students understand

that their first draft is like a block of marble. The idea is inside—it just needs shaping. Use phrases like: "What are you carving toward?" or "Where is the real image hiding?"
- **Walk through the sample poem slowly.** Read the before-and-after version aloud. Ask students what changed. How do the new lines feel different? Which tools are being used? This will help them develop an eye for poetic improvement.
- **Support emotional ownership.** When students identify the "heart" of their poem, let them choose what that means to them. One student's heart might be an image; another's might be a tone. There's no single correct answer.
- **Encourage risk.** If a student wants to revise their poem entirely from a new perspective, let them. Sometimes the best revision is a rewrite—and that's part of the process.
- **Reinforce selectivity.** They don't need to fix *everything* in one pass. Focus on one or two key areas: a single weak line, an unclear metaphor, or a muddled theme. They may only change a few words–that counts!!

One of the most important steps in writing poetry is revision.

Many writers assume that because a poem is short, it doesn't need much revision. But actually, because every word in a poem carries weight, revision is even more essential. The goal of revision is not just to make the poem better technically—it's to make it more powerful, more precise, and more poetic. In this lesson, we are going to look at the overall theme of your poem and consider ways to make it more precise.

Every poem begins with a spark: an idea, a memory, an emotion, or a moment. But the first draft is rarely the best way to express that spark. The process of revision is like sculpting. You begin with something rough, and you carve, smooth, and shape it until the true image appears. To do this, you need to ask yourself one central question: What is this poem really trying to say?

Start by identifying the heart of your poem. Read it over and ask: What is the emotion or message I want the reader to understand? Is it grief, joy, confusion, defiance, wonder? Try writing a single sentence that sums up what your poem is really about. For example, "This poem is about feeling lost after a friend moved away." Keep this sentence nearby as you revise.

Next, look at the tools you've used to communicate that idea. Did you use a metaphor? Did you rely on a strong image or a surprising phrase? Are you using repetition, contrast, or structure to guide the reader through your thought? If you're not sure, look back at the Tools of Poetry lesson and review what poetic tools are available. Then ask: which ones did I use well, and where could I use them more effectively? NOTE: We are going to work on this throughout our lessons, so you will know how to do this even better as we revise throughout the course.

The best thing you can do in the revision process is not hold too tightly to your work. Poems begin in your experience, but they are not supposed to report your exact experience—they are not written to truthfully tell a reality, but to be poems. It is in the revision process that they truly become poetry.

Here is an example of a first draft:

> The room is quiet
> except for the ticking clock.
> I sit on the edge of my bed
> waiting for the day to start.
> Outside, a car drives past.
> I don't move.

This version isn't bad—it gives us an image and a feeling. But it uses a lot of rather mundane or everyday images and ideas. Let's look at the lines to see if there is a better way to say some of these things. What happens in the revision?

> The walls hold their breath

while the clock paces.
I perch on the edge
of unfinished dreams.
A car sighs past the window.
I do not follow.

Now, the poet focuses on the theme of waiting and uncertainty. The room isn't just quiet–it "holds its breath." The clock doesn't just tick, it "paces." The narrator doesn't just sit, but rather "perches." The poem uses personification to deepen the emotional resonance. This is the kind of transformation that can happen when you ask: What is the most important part of this poem, and how can I sharpen it?

During revision, it's also helpful to think about whether your poetic choices are accidental or intentional. Did you choose a word just because it sounded pretty, or because it carried the exact meaning you needed? Did you break the line where you did because it looked good, or because it shaped the meaning of that moment?

A good way to evaluate this is to highlight one line you think is working really well and one line you think could be stronger. Ask: What is this strong line doing that makes it effective? Does it surprise the reader, create a vivid picture, or use a poetic tool well? Then, for the weaker line, ask: What's missing? Is it too vague? Too plain? Off-topic? Try rewriting just that one line using a poetic tool.

Revision is about asking questions, making choices, and shaping your words into something stronger than what you began with. This week, focus on identifying your poem's core message, selecting the right poetic tools, and using them with purpose. Don't try to fix everything at once. Just make it better than it was before—more focused, more vivid, more poetic. That's the art of revision.

Lesson 2 Activity: Revise Your Poems

Purpose of the Activity:

This revision activity helps students return to their earlier drafts with a focused mindset. Rather than reworking everything, they'll choose one key idea from each poem to strengthen. This structured, low-pressure revision encourages students to reflect on theme, evaluate their use of poetic tools, and revise one line with greater intentionality. It reinforces the idea that revision is about shaping meaning—not just correcting errors—and gives students a clear process they can use with future writing.

NOTE: It's okay if the student doesn't fix everything or fully understand their poetic options at this point. The final activity offers them an opportunity to return to these early poems for a second look.

Have the student complete the activity on their own, or use the guided learning together,

Guided Learning: How to Review with Students:

1. **Identify the core idea.**

    For each poem, students write one sentence that explains the central message, image, or emotion they want the poem to communicate. This helps them clarify their intention and guides the rest of the revision.

2. **Highlight the strongest line.**

    Students identify one line that supports that central idea most clearly. This gives them a success to build from and helps them recognize when a poetic choice is working well.

3. **Target one line for revision.**

    Next, students find a line that feels off-theme, vague, or less effective. This could be a line that's too plain, confusing, or unrelated to the poem's message.

4. **Revise using a poetic tool.**

    Students rewrite the weaker line using a new poetic technique—such as metaphor, a strong image, or other technique. Encourage students to try more than one

version before deciding which works best.
5. **(Optional) Peer or family feedback.**
   If possible, have students read their poem aloud to someone else and ask two questions:
   - What do you think this poem is about?
   - Which word or line could be more specific or vivid?

This step reinforces the idea that poetry is written to be read—and that feedback is part of the creative process.

Scoring Options:

Traditional Grading: Use the "Poem Revision" Rubric found in Appendix A. Review their poem revisions as a group on one rubric. This activity is worth 25 points.

Benchmark Grading: This activity is worth 25 points. Award all the points if they reflect on and revise at least one poem.

Let's look at the concepts we worked on this week and revise your poems. For this activity, focus on these things. For each of your three poems:

- Write one sentence that explains the central emotion, image, or idea in your poem.
- Highlight or star one line that captures this clearly.
- Now, find one line that doesn't support it—or feels off-theme.
- Revise that weaker line by trying a different tool (e.g., turn it into a metaphor, a new idea, or a vivid image).

Optional: The revision process works best with a partner–a parent, sibling, or friend. Have them read your poem and ask them:

- What do you think the theme of this poem is?
- What word or line do you think I could make more specific to help make this theme clear?

UNIT 2: STRUCTURING POETRY

In this unit, you'll learn how poets use line breaks and stanzas to shape the way a poem looks, sounds, and feels. You'll experiment with where to end a line and how to group lines into stanzas to guide the rhythm, meaning, and pace of your poem. You'll also learn how to revise your poem's structure—changing the layout without changing the words—to create different effects. These tools will help you build poems that are not only meaningful but also memorable.

Unit Objective:

Students will understand how line breaks and stanza structure affect the pacing, tone, and meaning of a poem. They will experiment with shaping their poems visually and rhythmically to create stronger emotional and artistic impact.

Unit Overview:

This unit introduces students to structure as a poetic tool—not just how a poem *looks* on the page, but how that visual structure shapes how it *sounds* and *feels*. Students will learn to recognize that every line break creates a pause, every stanza shift signals a turn, and even white space has meaning. Through guided practice and creative writing, they'll discover how to break lines with intention and group ideas into meaningful stanzas. This helps students begin to shape their poetry with rhythm, flow, and control.

Encourage students to read their poems aloud throughout this unit. Listening to their line breaks and stanza choices is one of the best ways to hear what's working—and what might need to change.

Lesson 3: Line Breaks & Stanzas

Objective:

Students will understand how line breaks and stanza structure affect the pacing, rhythm, meaning, and emotional impact of a poem. They will be able to identify types of line breaks and experiment with shaping their own poems using intentional breaks and stanza groupings.

Overview:

This lesson introduces students to two essential tools of poetic structure: line breaks and stanza formation. Rather than focusing on strict poetic forms, students explore the freedom poets have to shape how a poem *moves*—both visually and rhythmically. Through annotated examples and side-by-side comparisons, students will learn the effects of different line endings, and how different stanza choices impact meaning and tone.

Content Review:

Before beginning this lesson, review the idea from Unit 1 that *poetry is made from choices*. Ask students to recall how poetic tools help shape their meaning. Remind them that structure is another tool: poets decide where to place each line and each break. Highlight that changing and revising their own poems in Unit 1 to improve their theme was sometimes achieved by the structure of the poem itself.

Teaching Notes:

- **Begin with the mystery of line breaks.** Most students aren't taught how to break a line—they just write until they hit the margin. Let them know that *poets choose where to break the line*, and that choice matters deeply. Introduce the idea that each line break is a kind of "breath" in the poem.
- **Use the side-by-side examples as a read-aloud exercise.** The two versions of the same poem help students

hear how meaning shifts based on where a line ends. Ask: What do we notice in Version A vs. Version B? Which feels faster, heavier, more mysterious?
- **Clearly define end-stopped vs. enjambment.** Use Shakespeare's and Eliot's poems to show how punctuation—or lack of it—changes flow. Activity A will practice this idea.
- **Discuss stanzas as poetic "paragraphs."** Emphasize that stanza breaks guide the reader through shifts in thought, tone, or image. Ask students to compare the *structured* stanzas of Frost with the *varied* ones in Angelou and Williams. How do the stanzas control the energy of each poem?
- **Focus on *function*, not rules.** While this lesson introduces definitions and examples, the goal is not to memorize types—but to understand that form supports meaning. Encourage students to ask: *Why might the poet have broken the line or stanza here? What does that choice do for the poem?*
- **Encourage experimentation.** Let students know they'll be trying their own line breaks and stanza structures in the activity that follows. This is a chance to *play* with form, not perfect it.

Poetry Lines

One of the mysteries of poetry is where and when to put a line break. While some poems have a specific structure, most don't, and where to stop and start each line is up to you. But there are a few things to keep in mind with making these decisions—where you end your lines really does matter!

A **line of poetry** is a group of words that are collected together on one line of the paper. It ends when the poet wants it to end, not where the edge of the paper stops. A line can have one word or many words, and it can end with punctuation or not—all that is up to the poet.

The same few lines can feel completely different depending on where the break goes. Here's an example:

Poem Version A:
She ran through the fog
toward something
she couldn't see.

This version feels like it has a slower pacing, and created a sense of mystery and tension–in the first line, we are focused on "fog" and how she couldn't see.

Poem Version B:
She ran
through the fog toward something
she couldn't see.

Notice how changing that first line now makes the focus her action (running) rather than the fog. This creates a sense of urgency and faster pacing, perhaps even danger.

Types of Line Breaks

Always, at the end of each line, there exists a brief pause. The pause is what creates motion in a poem, a step in the dance of the word. *Where* you put that pause matters.

There are two types of line breaks: end-stopped and enjamb.

An **end-stopped line** is a line that ends in punctuation (a comma, period, comma, or explanation point).

Shall I compare thee to a summer's day?

Thou art more lovely and more temperate.
Rough winds do shake the darling buds of May,
And summer's lease hath all too short a date.
—from "Sonnet 18," William Shakespeare

The purpose of an end-stopped line is to give a rhythmic effect, or to end the thought. You slow down at punctuation, so it helps create pacing. An end-stopped line gives the sense of a completed thought within that line. NOTE: Some poets don't use the punctuation, but it is still considered an end-stopped line because it is considered to be a complete thought or phrase (the feeling of end-stop would not lessen, for example, in the poem above if the comma was left out after "May" above).

An **enjambment**, or "ending with an enjamb" is a line that does not end with any punctuation AND continues the thought into the next line. "Enjamb" is French for "crossing over."

April is the cruelest month, breeding
Lilacs out of the dead land, mixing
Memory and desire, stirring
Dull roots with spring rain.
Winter kept us warm, covering
Earth in forgetful snow, feeding
A little life with dried tubers.
—from "The Waste Land," TS Eliot

The purpose of an enjambment is to speed up a poem or emphasize a word for comic or emotional effect. It can also help explain complex thoughts across more than one line. NOTE: when you use enjambment, you can still use punctuation, just not at the end of the line.

Let's look again at Eliot's excerpt. How would the poem change if it had been written like this:

April is the cruelest month,

Breeding lilacs out of the dead land,
Mixing memory and desire,
Stirring dull roots with spring rain.

It changes the meaning, doesn't it? If you look again at the original, he ends every line with an action verb (breeding, mixing, stirring)—this creates a sense of movement, and focuses on the act of growth. When the lines are changed, look at how the focus becomes about cruelty, death, and dull roots. What you put at the end of a line matters!

These types of line breaks help us see that you can break a line *anywhere*, not just at the end of the sentence!

Stanzas of Poetry

A **stanza of poetry** is a collection of lines deliberately put together in a group. There are no spaces between the lines of a stanza, but there IS a space between each stanza in a poem. Some poems only have one stanza, while others can have hundreds. John Milton's famous poem *Paradise Lost* is an epic poem with over 10,000 lines broken up into only ten stanzas!

A stanza of poetry is like a paragraph in a story—it helps organize ideas or images. Poets use stanzas to group related lines together, often to create a pause, shift the mood, or highlight a new part of the poem.

Stanzas can be short or long, and they don't have to be the same length throughout the poem. Some poets keep their stanzas the same on purpose (like three lines per stanza, or four), while others change them to match the feeling of each section.

Here is an example of a very structured stanza poem–each stanza has four lines, and the lines rhyme (lines 1&4 and 2&3 rhyme, written as having a rhyme scheme of abba)

Stopping By Woods on a Snowy Evening
By Robert Frost

Whose woods these are I think I know.
His house is in the village though;
He will not see me stopping here
To watch his woods fill up with snow.

My little horse must think it queer
To stop without a farmhouse near
Between the woods and frozen lake
The darkest evening of the year.

He gives his harness bells a shake
To ask if there is some mistake.
The only other sound's the sweep
Of easy wind and downy flake.

The woods are lovely, dark and deep,
But I have promises to keep,
And miles to go before I sleep,
And miles to go before I sleep.

Try reading this poem out loud and listening for the pauses between stanzas. Do they feel like a new thought? A new scene?

And here is a poem with varied lengths of stanzas and lines, but it still rhymes! Notice how the repeated line throughout almost all the stanzas helps create the different scenes in the poem.

Life Doesn't Frighten Me
By Maya Angelou

Shadows on the wall
Noises down the hall
Life doesn't frighten me at all
Bad dogs barking loud
Big ghosts in a cloud
Life doesn't frighten me at all

Mean old Mother Goose
Lions on the loose
They don't frighten me at all

Dragons breathing flame
On my counterpane
That doesn't frighten me at all.

I go boo
Make them shoo
I make fun
Way they run
I won't cry
So they fly
I just smile
They go wild

Life doesn't frighten me at all.

Tough guys fight
All alone at night
Life doesn't frighten me at all.

Panthers in the park
Strangers in the dark
No, they don't frighten me at all.

That new classroom where
Boys all pull my hair
(Kissy little girls
With their hair in curls)
They don't frighten me at all.

Don't show me frogs and snakes
And listen for my scream,
If I'm afraid at all

It's only in my dreams.

I've got a magic charm
That I keep up my sleeve
I can walk the ocean floor
And never have to breathe.

Life doesn't frighten me at all
Not at all
Not at all.

Life doesn't frighten me at all.

And this one has equal lines in the stanzas, but no rhyme–and some of the lines consist of only one word!

This is Just to Say
By William Carlos Williams

I have eaten
the plums
that were in
the icebox
and which
you were probably
saving
for breakfast
Forgive me
they were delicious
so sweet
and so cold

Notice how the choices here really highlight the words, and leaves us with some interesting questions: he enjoyed the plums, but does he feel guilty that he ate them? Does he think the owner of the icebox will be mad...or maybe a little upset? Is that what "so cold" is referring to–both the plums, and the annoyed "coldness" of his partner? We don't know, but the way he formulates the words makes us consider ideas that are possibly underneath the statements.

Playing with your stanzas can change how we read a poem as much as the line can. Stanzas can help a poem feel orderly, chaotic, rhythmic (like a song), or fragmented.

Why Do Poets Play with Line Breaks and Stanzas?

Line breaks and stanza choices do more than make a poem "look" poetic. They help shape how the reader *feels* the poem.

Poets use line breaks to:
- Control pacing (fast or slow)
- Highlight important words
- Build suspense or surprise
- Organize ideas or images
- Emphasize emotion or rhythm

Stanza breaks work similarly, often giving extra emphasis to the last line (or word). Stanzas that break patterns can also help emphasize or highlight an idea. Every time you choose where to end a line or stanza, you're making a decision about what to spotlight.

Lesson 3 Activity A: Line Break Poem

Purpose of the Activity:

This activity helps students see how *line breaks alone* can turn everyday language into poetry. By starting with ordinary sentences and reshaping them into poems—without changing a single word—students discover the power of pacing, emphasis, and line arrangement. This activity reinforces the idea that poems aren't defined by rhyme or fancy vocabulary, but by *how* words are placed on the page. It also builds confidence by showing that poetic material can come from anywhere—even a text, email, or homework assignment.

Have the students complete the activity on their own use the guided learning together,

Guided Learning

1. **Introduce the premise.**

    Let students know they'll be transforming everyday sentences into poems—no new words required. The focus is 100% on line breaks. Explain that poets often begin with raw language—notes, thoughts, overheard phrases—and shape those into art through revision and structure.

2. **Collect a starting text.**

    Students choose 1–3 sentences they've written *outside* of poetry. This could be:
    - A line from a school paper
    - A text or message
    - A note to a parent
    - A caption or comment
    - Or (if nothing else) a few made-up sentences to a grandparent about why they're beautiful

    Total word count should be no more than 75 words to keep the activity focused.

3. **Prepare the raw version.**

   Students write out the original sentences *exactly as they were written*, along with a note about where the lines came from. (Example: "From a note I wrote to my sister.")

4. **Create Poem #1.**

   Students format the exact same words into a poem by adding line breaks wherever they choose. They should consider:
   - Where do I want the reader to pause?
   - What word do I want to emphasize at the end of each line?
   - How can line breaks change how the poem feels or sounds?

5. **Create Poem #2**

   Students start again, using the *same words*, but breaking the lines in a completely different way. The two poems should feel different—even though the language is the same. Each version gets a different title.

6. **Reflect (written or discussion).**

   Once both poems are complete, ask:
   - Which version feels more emotional, surprising, or clear?
   - How did changing the line breaks change the meaning?
   - What did you learn about structure just by moving words around?

Scoring Options:

Traditional Grading: Use the "Poem First Draft" Rubric found in Appendix A. In the tools section, focus on the variety of the line breaks in version 1 vs. version 2. This poem is worth 20 points.

Benchmark Grading: This poem is worth 20 points. Award 10 points for completing each version of this poem.

Find ONE to THREE sentences (no more than 75 words total for all the sentences) that you wrote for some other reason. It can be from a paper you wrote, a Facebook or Instagram status, an email, a note you wrote to your mom...anything at all. It just can't be a poem.

If you can't find anything, write three sentences to your Grandma about what makes her beautiful.

Then take those sentences and put them into poetic form. Mess around with line breaks and see what meaning you can create.

Create TWO poems out of the sentences you found. The words in both poems should be **exactly the same**; the only thing you are changing are the line breaks.

When you post your poems:
- Post the original sentences and say where you got them.
- Post your TWO poems—same words, different line break spots!
- Give each poem a different name.

Student Example (Shivaanshi P., age 14)

Original lines: He hated how small he felt. He stood there, staring at his brother. He looked like a ghost, but he was still breathing.

Poem 1: What He Saw
He hated
How small he felt
He stood there
Staring at his brother
He looked like a ghost
But
He was still breathing

Poem 2: "Still breathing"

He hated how
Small he felt
He stood there, staring

At his brother he looked
Like a ghost
But he was
Still breathing

Lesson 3 Activity B: One-Sentence Poem

Purpose of the Activity:

This activity helps students see how *line breaks alone* can turn everyday language into poetry. By starting with ordinary sentences and reshaping them into poems—without changing a single word—students discover the power of pacing, emphasis, and line arrangement. This activity reinforces the idea that poems aren't defined by rhyme or fancy vocabulary, but by *how* words are placed on the page. It also builds confidence by showing that poetic material can come from anywhere—even a text, email, or homework assignment.

Have the students complete the activity on their own use the guided learning together,

Guided Learning

1. **Introduce the premise.**

    Let students know they'll be transforming everyday sentences into poems—no new words required. The focus is 100% on line breaks. Explain that poets often begin with raw language—notes, thoughts, overheard phrases—and shape those into art through revision and structure.

2. **Collect a starting text.**

    Students choose 1–3 sentences they've written *outside* of poetry. This could be:
    - A line from a school paper
    - A text or message
    - A note to a parent
    - A caption or comment
    - Or (if nothing else) a few made-up sentences to a grandparent about why they're beautiful

Total word count should be no more than 75 words to keep the activity focused.

3. **Prepare the raw version.**

   Students write out the original sentences *exactly as they were written*, along with a note about where the lines came from. (Example: "From a note I wrote to my sister.")

4. **Create Poem #1.**

   Students format the exact same words into a poem by adding line breaks wherever they choose. They should consider:
   - Where do I want the reader to pause?
   - What word do I want to emphasize at the end of each line?
   - How can line breaks change how the poem feels or sounds?

5. **Create Poem #2.**

   Students start again, using the *same words*, but breaking the lines in a completely different way. The two poems should feel different—even though the language is the same. Each version gets a different title.

6. **Reflect (written or discussion).**

   Once both poems are complete, ask:
   - Which version feels more emotional, surprising, or clear?
   - How did changing the line breaks change the meaning?
   - What did you learn about structure just by moving words around?

Scoring Options:

Traditional Grading: Use the "Poem First Draft" Rubric found in Appendix A. In the tools section, focus on the variety of the line breaks in version 1 vs. version 2. This poem is worth 20 points.

Benchmark Grading: This poem is worth 20 points. Award 10 points for completing each version of this poem.

Create a poem that is only one sentence. Use the following poems by William Carlos Williams as examples. Here are the rules:

- Choose a person, animal, or moving object that is performing an action.
- The whole poem can only be one sentence.
- Each stanza should be composed of smaller distinct actions.
- Imitate the style or stanza lengths of any of the example poems.

Wedding Dance in the Open Air

Disciplined by the artist
to go round
and round

in holiday gear
a riotously gay rabble of
peasants and their

ample-bottomed doxies
fills
the market square

featured by the women in
their starched
white headgear

they prance or go openly
toward the wood's
edges

round and around in
rough shoes and
farm breeches

mouths agape
Oya !
kicking up their heels

The Red Wheelbarrow

so much depends
upon

a red wheel
barrow

glazed with rain
water

beside the white
chickens.

This Is Just To Say

I have eaten
the plums
that were in
the icebox

and which
you were probably
saving
for breakfast

Forgive me
they were delicious
so sweet
and so cold.

Lesson 3 Activity C: Line Builder Poem

Purpose of the Activity:
This activity helps students build a poem from the ground up by generating 12 original lines based on flexible, image-rich prompts. Once the lines are written, the focus shifts to *structure*: how the lines are grouped and arranged into stanzas. This two-part process lets students practice both poetic content and form. It encourages play, reflection, and deeper understanding of how stanza shape can influence tone, pacing, and emphasis.

Have the students complete the activity on their own use the guided learning together,

Guided Learning

1. **Begin with guided line generation.**
   Students are given 12 open-ended prompts to help them create the raw material for a poem. Emphasize that these don't have to be "poetic" yet—just detailed, sensory, and honest. You can model a few example lines as needed or use the example in the exercise

2. **Complete all 12 lines.**
   Before moving on, check that each student has completed all 12 lines. These can be short or long, complete sentences or fragments. The important thing is that they are *their own words*—drawn from observation, imagination, or memory.

3. **Prepare the lines for experimentation (optional but highly recommended)**
   - Have students write or type/print just their answers (not the prompts) on a piece of paper with space between them. Then cut the paper up so that each slip of paper contains only one line. Let the students complete steps #3 and #4 by physically manipulating their lines on a table until they find a structure they like.

4. **Introduce the idea of structure experimentation.**
   Let students know they'll now turn their 12 lines into a

poem by *only* rearranging line breaks and stanzas—no changing the words. Encourage them to think of this like cutting up the same message and taping it back together in different shapes.

5. **Choose and test stanza patterns.**
   Students experiment with **at least two different stanza structures**, such as:
   - Three stanzas of 4 lines each
   - Four stanzas of 3 lines each
   - Two stanzas of 6 lines
   - Uneven stanzas–they can have a one-line stanza or 3 lines, then 5 lines, then two lines, etc

Encourage them to experiment and try different layouts—what effect does the grouping create?

Once they are satisfied with their order, record their final layout in the workbook.

Scoring Options:

Traditional Grading: Use the "Poem First Draft" Rubric found in Appendix A. In the tools section, focus on following the activity requirements and having colorful lines arranged in interesting stanzas. This poem is worth 20 points.

Benchmark Grading: This poem is worth 20 points. Award 10 points for completing each version of this poem.

In this activity, you'll build your own poem using lines you create—with a little help to get you started. Then you'll explore how grouping those lines into stanzas changes the feel of your poem.

Step 1: Fill in the blanks below with your own ideas.

Don't worry about being poetic yet—just be descriptive! You can write complete sentences or a phrase. (Example: For #3, I could write " a low, long train whistle" or "a train whistle in the distance" or "A lonely train whistle echoes across the hills")

1. Something the sky is doing: _____

2. A small object you notice outdoors: _____

3. A sound you hear or imagine: _____

4. A person or animal doing something: _____

5. A color and a noun: _____

6. Something you feel (emotion or physical): _____

7. A question you might ask your best friend: _____

8. A movement or action: _____

9. Something surprising or strange: _____

10. Something you see out of the corner of your eye: _____

11. A smell in the air: _____

12. Something that has been left behind after a picnic: _____

Step 2: Arrange your 12 lines into stanzas.

Take each of the lines above and arrange them into a poem with several stanzas.

Recommendation: Type (or write) each of these lines, print them out, and cut them up so you have one line on each slip of paper. Physically rearrange them until you come up with a layout you like.

Try out different stanza groupings. Here are three options you can experiment with:
- Three stanzas of four lines each
- Four stanzas of three lines each
- Two stanzas of six lines each
- Stanzas of uneven numbers of lines

Lesson 4: Revising Structures

Objective:

Students will revise their poems by analyzing and adjusting line breaks and stanza structure. They will make intentional decisions about visual layout, pacing, and rhythm in order to enhance the poem's emotional flow and clarity.

Overview:

This lesson encourages students to see structure as a poetic tool—not just a formatting choice. By returning to a previously written poem, students will experiment with rearranging lines, breaking stanzas differently, and reading their work aloud to hear how each version affects the pacing and tone.

Content Review:

Before beginning this lesson, review key concepts from Lesson 3 about the purpose of line breaks and stanzas. Remind students that each line break creates a pause and that stanza changes often signal shifts in thought, image, or tone. Revisit the poem examples from Angelou and Williams, or the side-by-side line break exercises. Ask students to describe how the *same words* felt different when arranged differently. Then explain that today's goal is to apply that same awareness to their own work.

Teaching Notes:

- **Read the student example aloud.** Start the lesson by reading the "Figure Skate Carved" poem aloud in both versions. Ask students: *What changed? Which version felt smoother or more dramatic? What might the revised structure emphasize that the first draft didn't?*
- **Highlight the idea of experimentation.** Let students know they're not locked into any one structure. Encourage them to try out multiple formats: couplets, tercets, one-word lines, or no stanza breaks at all.
- **Use strong vs. weak line endings.** Reinforce the strategy of ending lines on *strong* words (nouns, verbs, striking

adjectives). Show examples of how a weak line ending (e.g., "and," "of," "was") can flatten a line—unless it's being used intentionally for effect.

- **Encourage reading aloud.** The best way to evaluate line breaks and rhythm is to *listen* to the poem. Prompt students to read both versions of their poem aloud and ask: *Which version moves the way I want it to?*
- **Invite student choice.** Remind students that structure is personal. There's no "correct" version—only the version that best matches the feeling or message they want to convey.
- **Keep revisions focused.** They don't need to rewrite the whole poem. One rearranged stanza or a few shifted line breaks can dramatically change the feel of the piece.

Poetry is not just what we say—it's how we say it. And one of the most important ways we shape meaning in a poem is through line breaks and stanza structure. In this lesson, we'll focus on how to revise your poem by considering where each line ends, how lines are grouped, and how the visual layout on the page supports the feeling or rhythm of the piece.

Line breaks aren't just there to make a poem look pretty. Each break creates a pause, even a small one, and that pause adds meaning. Ending a line on a strong word (a noun or verb) pulls the reader forward. Ending a line on a weak or filler word (like "of" or "and") might weaken the impact—unless you're doing it for effect.

Stanzas, too, have their own power. They are visual and emotional containers. A stanza can mark a shift in time, tone, or thought. Even the choice to use no stanzas at all communicates something about the emotional flow of the poem.

When revising, ask yourself: Why did I break the line where I did? What happens when I move that line break? Does each stanza feel complete, or does it trail off? Could I group these lines differently to emphasize a change in thought or emotion?

Let's look at a student example.

First Draft:

The Figure Skate Carved
By Shivaanshi P., age 14

A silver line
Into frozen ice
So clean
It caught
The light
And held
Its breath

Before spinning
Softly
Into
silence.

Teacher Revision Suggestion:
I think the last line should be "Into silence" rather than having them break so that it matches the last line of the first two stanzas.
OR

You could play with these and adjust the third line of stanza one to have three words ("So sharply clean"?), then cut "Before" in the third stanza, and then you have a really cool three word-two word-one word stanza structure!

Revised Version:

The Figure Skate Carved
By Shivaanshi P., age 14

A silver line
Into frozen ice
So clean

It caught
The light
And held

Its breath
Before spinning
Softly

Into silence.

In this case, the student liked the first idea rather than the second, because she wanted the "Into silence" to have the weight after the one-word of "softly." That is absolutely her right as the poet to choose!

Your own poem might benefit from a similar experiment. Try rewriting it with one of these approaches:
- Break each sentence into two or three shorter lines.
- Make each stanza a separate moment or image.

- End each line on a strong word (noun, verb, or striking adjective).

Then read both versions aloud. Which one helps your reader move with your poem the way you want them to? Which structure better matches your poem's emotional rhythm?

Remember, structure can be subtle. It doesn't always shout. But when you use line breaks and stanzas intentionally, your poem gains power. It reads more like music and less like a journal entry. Each break becomes a breath, a beat, a brushstroke that helps your meaning land more clearly.

In this revision stage, don't be afraid to play. Structure is something you can change again and again until it fits. Try a block of text. Then try couplets. Try one-word lines. Then something more traditional. Pay attention to how it *feels* when you read it out loud.

Revising your poem's structure means thinking about how line breaks and stanzas shape the reader's experience. Be intentional. Use form to match feeling. These changes don't need to be big—moving one word or one line break can be all it takes.

Ask yourself not just what your poem says—but *how* it moves.

Lesson 4 Activity

Purpose of the Activity:
This activity invites students to return to one or more of their poems and focus solely on structure. By reworking line breaks and stanza groupings, students learn how form influences flow, tone, and emotional emphasis. This revision process builds awareness of how visual choices shape the reader's experience and gives students space to test and compare different structures before deciding what works best for their poem.

Have the student complete the worksheet independently, or work through the guided learning below together

Guided Learning:
1. **Choose a poem (or more).**

    Students may revise one, two, or all three poems written in this unit. Encourage them to choose the one they feel most connected to—or the one that "feels off" structurally.

2. **Ask guiding questions.**

    Before revising, students reflect on the following:
    - Where do my lines currently break—and why?
    - Do the stanza groupings feel natural or forced?
    - Does the structure support the poem's rhythm and emotional arc?

3. **Rewrite using different structure.**

    Students rewrite the chosen poem using a different stanza format or breaking lines in new places. They may test out couplets, long stanzas, or uneven groupings—whatever feels most effective. Remind them: the *words stay the same*, but the *shape* of the poem changes.

4. **(Optional) Share with a partner.**

    If possible, students read their revised version to a peer, family member, or friend and ask the questions found at the end of the activity.

Scoring Options:

Traditional Grading: Use the "Poem Revision" Rubric found in Appendix A. Review their poem revisions as a group on one rubric. This activity is worth 25 points.

Benchmark Grading: This activity is worth 25 points. Award all the points if they reflect on and revise at least one poem.

Choose one, two, or all three of your poems in this unit to restructure. As you revise, consider the following questions:
- Where do your lines break—and why?
- Do your stanza groupings make sense or add emotional weight?
- Does anything feel too choppy or too blocky?

Rewrite your poems here with different line breaks or stanzas as needed to create more meaning.

Star the choice that you like the best.

Optional: The revision process works best with a partner–a parent, sibling, or friend. Have them read your poem and ask them:
- Do the line breaks and stanzas look right?
- Are there changes to the structure I could make to create more meaning?

UNIT 3: SOUND QUALITY

In this unit, you'll learn how to make your poems come alive by paying attention to sound. Poets don't just choose words for meaning—they choose them for how they feel when spoken aloud. You'll explore tools like alliteration, repetition, rhythm, and rhyme, and see how sounds can shape the mood and energy of a poem. You'll also experiment with sound in playful ways and learn how to revise your poems to make them more musical and powerful. Whether your poem is loud and bouncy or soft and smooth, sound is what makes it sing.

Unit Objective:

Students will explore how sound shapes the mood, rhythm, and emotional resonance of a poem. They will learn to use tools such as alliteration, repetition, rhyme, and meter to enhance their poetic voice. By experimenting with sound devices and revising for clarity and flow, students will discover how sound transforms written words into living, expressive art.

Unit Overview:

In this unit, students will learn that poetry is not just about what is said—it's about *how* it sounds. Words carry rhythm, texture, and tone, and poets use sound to add emotion, energy, and emphasis to every line. Students will study examples of sound in classic and contemporary poetry, then write and revise their own poems with sound in mind. This unit encourages students to listen closely, experiment boldly, and revise with the ear as well as the eye. Whether their style is lyrical or playful, students will learn to make their poetry move and resonate.

Lesson 5: Sound Quality

Objective:

Students will identify and experiment with sound devices such as alliteration, assonance, consonance, repetition, onomatopoeia, rhyme, and meter. They will write original poems that emphasize sound, using deliberate choices to create rhythm, mood, and musicality.

Overview:

This lesson focuses on the *auditory* power of poetry. Students will explore how poets use sound not just for style but for substance—how the feel of words can mirror or enhance meaning. Through reading examples and completing guided writing prompts, students will develop an ear for rhythm and learn to shape their writing with sound. They'll also discover how different sound tools create different emotional tones: a bouncing rhyme might feel playful, while soft alliteration can feel dreamlike or melancholy. Students will have opportunities to create poems that range from silly to serious—all while strengthening their awareness of how sound shapes language.

Content Review:

Before beginning this lesson, review the importance of line breaks and stanza structure from Unit 2. Remind students that structure affects pacing, and that sound works alongside structure to enhance meaning. Ask students to recall how short lines, long stanzas, or sudden breaks affected how a poem moved. Now, explain that we're shifting focus to *what fills those lines*—specifically, the sounds inside the words themselves. Let students know they'll now explore tools that help control the *soundtrack* of their poem.

Teaching Notes:

- **Anchor the lesson in listening.** Explain that poetry is meant to be *heard*. Encourage students to read everything aloud—examples, their own drafts, even nonsense

- phrases—to develop their ear.
- **Define and compare sound tools clearly.** Use the chart provided in the student text to break down terms like alliteration, rhythm, and onomatopoeia. But remember, the goal is to get them to *use* these techniques, not simply to be able to define them.
- **Demonstrate with examples.** Read from the poems by Coleridge, Tennyson, Poe, and Lawrence. Ask students what they hear and how the sound contributes to mood. Use phrases like: *What do you feel when you hear that repeated "m" sound?*
- **Encourage play.** Let students know that this unit includes both *serious* and *nonsense* poetry. Playful experimentation builds awareness. It's okay to invent words, bend rhythm, or exaggerate sound effects. That's part of learning.
- **Model meter and rhyme with familiar examples.** Use Dr. Seuss and Shakespeare to show how rhythm (or broken rhythm) changes how a poem feels. Clap the beat or tap your desk to help students "hear" the pattern.
- **Don't require rhyme.** Remind students that rhyme is optional—it's one tool, not the goal. The focus is on *deliberate* sound, not forced rhyming.
- **Use group brainstorming.** For warm-up, try a class sound scavenger hunt: "What's a word that sounds joyful? Harsh? Quiet? Loud?" This helps students connect sound to tone before writing.

There are several ways that poets play with the way words sound to create a meaning and rhythm when the poem is read aloud. Many times it is done to create emotional power, even when reading (it's hard to read "Peter picked a peck of pickled peppers" without hearing that forceful "p" sound isn't it?). There are several different ways this is done. Sound isn't just music—it's emotion. Smooth vowel sounds can feel peaceful. Hard consonants can feel angry or energetic. Listen to your poem as much as you read it.

Choosing Words Because of How They Sound

Part of writing poetry is word choice—we have so many words in the English language to choose from. If we want to say that the elephant was big, for example, we could say it was giant, huge, gargantuan, massive, or colossal. Those are all great words! But if we are writing a poem, we could pick one that creates a sound: "enormous elephant." See how the two words both start with e, and that creates a different sound quality than "big elephant"? Or, we could look at the end of the word and write "giant elephant" to create a connection through that stomping t sound at the end. It all depends on how you want your poem to sound!

Here are some ways to play with your choice of words (and letters) to create continued word sounds:

Alliteration is repeating consonants to create a mood or emotion. Note how this line from Samuel Coleridge's "Kubla Khan" describing a river sounds like a slow-moving river because of the repeated "m" consonant sounds:

Five miles meandering with a mazy motion

Assonance is the repetition of similar vowel sounds. Just like with alliteration, it creates a mood. Read the following lines from Alfred, Lord Tennyson's "Lotus-Eaters" and listen to the drowsy, slow effect the long o and ou vowels create:

The Lotus blooms below the barren peak;
The Lotus blows by every winding creek:
All day the wind breaths low with the mellower tone
Thro' every hollow cave and ally lone,
Round and round the spicy downs the yellow Lotus-dust is blown.

Consonance is the repetition of consonants in words that are next to or close to each other. This may sound similar to alliteration, but consonance can occur in the middle or end of the word—not just the beginning.

Example:
It was ma**n**y a**n**d ma**n**y a year ago,
I**n** a ki**n**gdom by the sea,
That a maide**n** there **l**ived whom you may know
By the **n**ame of A**nn**abe**l** Lee;
And this maide**n** she **l**ived with **n**o other thought
Than to **l**ove and be **l**oved by me.
—"Annabel Lee," Edgar Allen Poe

Onomatopoeia is the use of words that imitate sounds. It can be as straightforward as "crack," "moo," or "pop," or it can be more subtle where the sounds of the words are deliberately used to reflect the sense of the lines. Look at the second stanza of D.H. Lawrence's poem "Snake" and pay attention to how the sounds of the letters work together to make you think of a snake moving:

He sipped with his straight mouth,
Softly drank through his straight gums, into his slack long body,
Silently.

Sound Device	What It Means	Example
Alliteration	Repeating consonants at the start of words	*Whispering winds whirled*

Assonance	Repeating vowel sounds	*The moon moved through gloom*
Consonance	Repeating consonant sounds (not just at the start)	*Blank and think*
Onomatopoeia	Words that imitate sound	*Buzz, snap, rustle*

Sound & Line Breaks: Tools for Creating Rhythm

Rhythm in music is the beat—it's the thing you clap along to when you listen to a song. Poems also have a **rhythm**, a beat or pace that we can feel as we read. In fact, all songs are actually poems set to music! Some poems have an obvious rhythm (like a Dr. Seuss book), and others deliberately break rhythm patterns to make words or ideas stand out. There are several things you can do to create a rhythm (or avoid creating a rhythm) in your poem.

Meter

One way to create this rhythm is with the syllables in a line. How you use syllables to accent certain sounds is called **meter**. Meter in song is called the "beat." Look at this line from William Shakespeare:

Shall I compare thee to a summer's day?

Do you hear the beat? One-TWO, three-FOUR, five-SIX, seven-EIGHT, nine-TEN. You can tap your foot along with it. But that beat changes if you switch the words around or use different endings:

Comparing thee to summer

This doesn't have the same meter. Dr. Seuss does the same

thing in his books:

One fish, two fish, red fish, blue fish.

It's a different meter than Shakespeare, but it has the same effect. It wouldn't read the same if it said:

Count the fish, red and blue.

Meter has many different styles and combinations, but all of them have to do with how your words create a rhythm. If a line doesn't sound "right" it might be because your meter is different in that line than the others in your poem—try switching the words around or changing the endings to create the same "beat" as the rest of your poem.

And remember, you are allowed to break all the rules of meter—these types of poems are called **free verse**, and they can't be sung or clapped along with any set "beat."

Repeating Words

Repetition is the using the same word or statement throughout a poem to create meaning or heighten the emotional impact. It could be a repeated word, like this speech from Shakespeare's Macbeth:

Tomorrow and tomorrow and tomorrow,
Creeps in this petty pace from day to day,

Or it could be a repeated line, like in "Do Not Go Gentle Into That Good Night" by Dylan Thomas, who repeats the title line four times in his 19 line poem.

Do not go gentle into that good night,
Old age should burn and rave at close of day;
Rage, rage against the dying of the light.

Though wise men at their end know dark is right,

Because their words had forked no lightning they
Do not go gentle into that good night.
Good men, the last wave by, crying how bright
Their frail deeds might have danced in a green bay,
Rage, rage against the dying of the light.

Wild men who caught and sang the sun in flight,
And learn, too late, they grieved it on its way,
Do not go gentle into that good night.

Grave men, near death, who see with blinding sight
Blind eyes could blaze like meteors and be gay,
Rage, rage against the dying of the light.

And you, my father, there on that sad height,
Curse, bless, me now with your fierce tears, I pray.
Do not go gentle into that good night.
Rage, rage against the dying of the light.

A **refrain** is a repeated series of lines that repeat throughout the poem. While repetition is when you repeat a word or phrase anywhere in the poem, refrain is a repeated **group of lines**—like the chorus of a song.

Rhyme

Beginning poets often think that a poem has to rhyme. This is simply not true. A rhyme is only one tool to create structure, not the only tool! A **rhyme** is when two words have corresponding sounds. This most commonly happens at the end of lines, but it can also be done in the middle of lines.

There are two types of rhymes. **Full (or perfect) rhyme** is when vowel and the following consonants rhyme (fish/dish, smiling/filing). **Slant (or half) rhyme** is when the vowels do not match, but the following consonants do (fish/dash, smiling/falling)

Rhyming can also occur in two places. It can be in the same line, called an **internal rhyme**, or it can be at the end of a line, called an **external rhyme**. Edgar Allan Poe uses both in his famous poem "The Raven":

Once upon a midnight <u>dreary</u>, while I pondered, weak and <u>weary</u>,
Over many a quaint and curious volume of forgotten **lore**—
While I nodded, nearly <u>napping</u>, suddenly there came a <u>tapping</u>,
As of some one gently <u>rapping</u>, <u>rapping</u> at my chamber **door**.
"'Tis some visitor," I muttered, "<u>tapping</u> at my chamber **door**—
Only this and nothing **more**."

When a poem has a regular pattern of external rhymes, we call that the poem's **rhyme scheme**. Usually, rhyme schemes are designated by letters (abab, aabb, abacada). Each letter corresponds to the end of the line—if the sound is the same, use the same letter. So for the verse above from "The Raven," the rhyme scheme would be abcbbb. The first three lines are different, so they get their own letters (a, b, and c). But the last three lines match the second line, so we use the letter that we assigned to it—b.

These patterns can be anything that a poet chooses, but certain types of poems have rhyme rules. A limerick has a rhyme pattern of aabba. A Shakespearean sonnet is more complicated and must follow the rhyme scheme of abab cdcd efef gg. Unless you are following a specific form, you are allowed to follow any rhyme scheme you like, or have none at all!

Lesson 5 Activity A: Random Words, Deliberate Sounds Poem

Purpose of the Activity:
This activity gives students a playful and creative way to apply sound devices to original poetry. By starting with five random words, students are challenged to shape a poem around sound rather than content alone. This encourages flexibility, creative risk-taking, and deeper attention to how word sounds influence tone, rhythm, and emotional effect. The seasonal theme provides just enough focus to keep the assignment grounded, while the sound tools open the door to experimentation.

Have the student complete the activity alone or complete it together using the guided learning.

Guided Learning

1. **Collect five random words.**

    Students should gather five words from an unexpected source—a magazine, cereal box, online article, or book. The more random, the better! The point is to work creatively with *whatever* language they are given.

2. **Choose a season to write about**

    Have students pick one season (spring, summer, fall, or winter) as the backdrop or mood for the poem. This gives the writing direction and imagery to build from.

3. **Review sound tools.**

    Before writing, quickly review the definitions and examples of sound devices from the lesson:
    - Alliteration
    - Assonance
    - Repetition
    - Rhyme

    Let students know they'll need to use at least two of these tools in their poem. Optional challenge: use three or more.

4. **Write the poem.**
   Students write a poem that includes all five random words and applies at least two sound devices. The words don't have to be the *focus*—they just need to appear somewhere in the poem. Encourage students to read aloud as they write to test rhythm and sound.
5. **Highlight sound techniques and random words.**
   Once complete, students underline or highlight the lines where they used alliteration, rhyme, or other sound devices. This reinforces recognition of how and where they used the tools. Have them circle their random words.
6. **Optional reflection or sharing.**
   Invite students to share their favorite sound from their poem or explain which random word was hardest to use. Ask: *How did the sound tools help shape your mood or season?*

Scoring Options:
Traditional Grading: Use the "Poem First Draft" Rubric found in Appendix A. In the tools section, focus on the sound quality. This poem is worth 20 points.
Benchmark Grading: This poem is worth 20 points. Award 10 points for completing the poem, 1 point each for having 5 random words, and 5 points each for including two techniques in the poem.

Pick five random words (from a magazine, book, online source, or cereal box). Then, write a poem about the changing of a season, and choose ***any two*** of the following devices to include in your poem:
- Make one of the words rhyme
- Use alliteration with one of the words
- Use assonance with one of the words
- Repeat one word (or line) for effect

Optional challenge: Try to include *three or more* of these sound tools in your poem.

Lesson 5 Activity B: Nonsense Poem

Purpose of the Activity:
This activity gives students permission to break free from logic and focus entirely on *sound, rhythm,* and *mood*. By creating their own nonsense words and pairing them with a deliberate emotional tone, students learn how language—even when it doesn't "mean" anything—can still communicate feeling. This is a low-pressure, high-creativity exercise that strengthens a poet's ear and builds confidence with sound-based tools like alliteration, assonance, and onomatopoeia.

Have the student complete the activity alone or complete it together using the guided learning.

Guided Learning: Directing the Process
1. **Introduce nonsense poetry.**
   Read the excerpt from "Jabberwocky" aloud and discuss how even though many of the words are made up, the meaning and emotion are clear. Ask: *How do the sounds help us know what's happening? How do nonsense words carry mood?*
2. **Generate original nonsense words.**
   Students create **at least five original nonsense words**, placing them into word categories (noun, verb, adjective, adverb). Encourage playfulness—students can combine real word parts or make up entirely new ones. Let them add endings like "-ly" or "-ing" to make the words fit their poem.
3. **Choose a mood.**
   Students select a specific mood from the provided list (e.g., anxious, silly, joyful, fearful). This mood becomes the *anchor* for their poem—it should guide the tone, energy, and rhythm of their writing.
4. **Write the poem.**
   Students write a short poem using their invented words to convey the chosen mood. The poem **does not need to**

make logical sense, but the tone should be recognizable. Encourage students to use sound devices like repetition, onomatopoeia, and alliteration to strengthen the emotional effect.

5. **Read aloud.**

    Once complete, students read their poem aloud. Ask: *Does it sound like the mood you intended? Which parts worked best?* Emphasize that clarity of feeling—not meaning—is the goal.

6. **Optional: Visual word bank.**

    If students need support generating nonsense words, let them use a dictionary flip or letter mash-up game. You can also model how to adapt a real word into nonsense form (e.g., "chatter" → "blatter," "jelly" → "jubby").

Scoring Options:

Traditional Grading: Use the "Poem First Draft" Rubric found in Appendix A. In the tools section, focus on the sound quality. This poem is worth 20 points.

Benchmark Grading: This poem is worth 20 points. Award 10 points for completing the poem, 1 point each for having 5 nonsense words, and 5 points for clearly communicating a tone.

The goal of this poem is to help you pay attention to the sound quality of words and ways you can create a mood with sounds. You need to let go of meaning—this is a mood poem.

One of the most famous poets to write nonsense poems is Lewis Carroll (the author of Alice in Wonderland). Here is an excerpt from his poem "Jabberwocky":

> And, as in uffish thought he stood,
>   The Jabberwock, with eyes of flame,
>   Came whiffling through the tulgey wood,
>   And burbled as it came!
> One, two! One, two! And through and through

> The vorpal blade went snicker-snack!
> He left it dead, and with its head
> He went galumphing back.

Notice the use of nonsense words (uffish, whiffling, tulgey, burbled, vorpal, snicker-snack, galumphing). Yet somehow, we know exactly what happened!

So here's how to create your nonsense poem:

1. Create your own nonsense words. You need to make up AT LEAST FIVE words. Organize them into nouns, verbs, adjectives, and adverbs. You ARE allowed to add endings (-s, -ly, -ment, -ing) as needed to make them work in your poem. (If you get stuck, get a dictionary and open it to any page and pick a weird word—change or add a few letters. Don't read the definitions, though!)
2. Pick a mood from this list.

Aggravated	Amused	Angry	Anxious
Apologetic	Ashamed	Blissful	Confused
Content	Determined	Discontent	Ecstatic
Envious	Excited	Exhausted	Fearful
Forgetful	Frustrated	Grateful	Grumpy
Guilty	Hopeful	Jealous	Joyful
Jubilant	Lonely	Melancholy	Mischievous
Rejected	Restless	Sad	Shocked
Sick	Silly	Surprised	Thankful

3. Write a poem creating the mood you picked in #2 with the words from #1. Remember, assonance and alliteration and onomatopoeia help communicate moods and emotions!
4. The poem does NOT need to make sense word-wise, but a reader should be able to understand the mood. It helps to choose your "noun" and have it do an action. Note how in the example above there are enough "normal" words to figure out the mood and what is going on.

Lesson 5 Activity C: Popping Popcorn Poem

Purpose of the Activity:

This activity teaches students how to translate real-world sound into poetic language. By observing a familiar event (like popcorn popping or rain falling) and listening closely, students learn to describe sounds through simile, metaphor, rhythm, and onomatopoeia. It builds sensory awareness and helps students discover that poetry is all around them—if they take the time to listen.

Have the student complete the activity alone or complete it together using the guided learning.

Guided Learning:

1. **Choose and complete a sound observation.**

    Students select one of the following real-life sounds listed in the activity to observe. They should sit quietly and **listen closely** with their eyes closed for several minutes, focusing only on the sounds.

2. **Record sound comparisons.**

    While listening, students write down **what each sound reminds them of**. Encourage them to use **similes or metaphors** (e.g., "like applause," "like a bouncing marble," "like someone whispering secrets"). They should write freely without trying to make full sentences.

3. **Draft a sound-based poem.**

    Using their sound list, students write a poem. The poem can follow any structure they like—each line might describe a different sound, or it might build toward a single moment. The goal is to **capture the rhythm, tone, and texture** of what they heard.

4. **Emphasize sound devices.**

    Encourage students to use:

- **Onomatopoeia** (e.g., pop, hiss, clink)
- **Repetition** for rhythm
- **Line breaks** that match the beat or motion of the sound

Remind them that this is a *sound-first* poem—the imagery should be driven by what they heard, not what they saw.

5. **Read aloud and reflect.**

   After writing, students read their poems aloud. Ask:
   - Which line feels the most like the sound you heard?
   - Did your rhythm or word choice change as you listened longer?
   - Which sounds were hardest to describe?

Scoring Options:

Traditional Grading: Use the "Poem First Draft" Rubric found in Appendix A. In the tools section, focus on the sound quality. This poem is worth 20 points.

Benchmark Grading: This poem is worth 20 points. Award 10 points for completing the poem, 1 point each for having 5 random words, and 5 points each for including two techniques in the poem.

For this poem, you need to do a little observation first. Choose one of the following activities to complete:
- Pop some popcorn (microwave or on the stove).
- Fill a jar halfway up with water and have a sibling or parent shake it fast and slow
- Turn on the dishwasher and sit next to it.
- Sit on your porch when it is raining.

While the action is happening above, close your eyes and listen. Try to pick out different sounds you hear. As you listen, write down things it sounds like. List as many things as you can.

Then write a poem that lists all of the sounds you heard. You can write this any way you like. You could create a verse that explains each sound you heard. You could write one line for each comparison. The possibilities are endless!

Storm

By Aiden L.

The static of water crackles in one's ears

A vacuum of void consumes everything around it

Constant crashing of tiny buildings

A machine gun onslaught that never ends

A fine mist descends upon the thunder

Calm repetitiveness in a chaotic storm

Popcorn!

By Noah L.

Pop pop pop pop pop

The popcorn is exploding

Pop pop pop pop stop.

Machine is empty

Sadly, no more corn to pop.

We ran out of corn.

We got some more corn!

Pop pop pop pop pop pop BOOM!

Machine exploded.

Way, way too much corn.

we need a new machine.

Kitchen overflowed.

Maybe made too much.

It's fine; we'll eat it all up

On second thought, don't.

Sounds of Water

By Alyssa W.

Gurgling, gurgling

Soft ripples

water slapping against the pebbles

pushing the verdant calamus

On the beach

with crystal clear water

on a cool sumemr day

where the waves only just

patter by her dangling feet

Deeper, deeper

breathing with life

Meditation in nature

Kids run on the wet sand

laughing, splashing, frolicking

The melody changing

Rumbling, rumbling
Heavy rain is coming
The fish pop out of the water to seek shelter
A frog jumps from the lotus leaf into the pond
Everything goes to peace
The calm before the storm

Lesson 6: Revising for Sound

Objective:

Students will revise one or more of their poems by listening closely to how their writing sounds when read aloud. They will apply sound-based revision techniques to improve rhythm, enhance flow, and strengthen emotional impact.

Overview

In this lesson, students take their sound-focused poems from Lesson 5 and revise them with the ear in mind. They'll concentrate on how their words *sound*—reading aloud, spotting awkward rhythms or flat phrases, and adjusting lines to better reflect the tone and energy they want. This revision process deepens students' control over language and shows them how even small word swaps or line changes can dramatically improve the musicality and power of a poem.

Content Review

Before beginning this lesson, review the main sound devices from Lesson 5:

- Alliteration, assonance, and consonance (repetition of sounds)
- Onomatopoeia (sound-imitating words)
- Repetition (for emphasis or rhythm)
- Meter and rhyme (creating beat and flow)

Remind students that these tools aren't just decorations—they help the poem land emotionally and musically. Ask: *Where in your poem did the sound match the feeling? Where did it fall flat?* This is their cue for revision.

Teaching Notes:

- **Start with read-alouds.** Emphasize that revision in this lesson starts with listening. Model how reading a poem aloud slowly and then again quickly can reveal pacing issues or word choices that feel "off."
- **Highlight problem areas.** Encourage students to *mark or*

underline lines that feel awkward or flat. These are the best places to revise. Let them know that good poets often revise *one word at a time*—precision is key.
- **Use sound tools deliberately.** Guide students to review the chart in Lesson 5 and ask if they could add any of these tools or revise to make them more effective.
- **Model a revision.** Read the "Popping Popcorn" student example aloud in both draft and revised forms. Ask students to identify what changed, and how the sound improved.
- **Encourage "ear editing."** Remind students that the *ear is often a better editor than the eye*. If it sounds awkward, it likely needs a change—even if the words are technically fine.
- **Keep revision focused.** Students don't need to revise every line. If they revise 2–3 lines well, that's a major win in sound control. Notice in the example, she only added two words so that the sound of the stanzas aligned better.
- **Invite peer or family input.** If possible, encourage students to share their poem with a listener who can offer feedback on rhythm and flow. A fresh ear often catches what the writer can't hear.

Sound is one of poetry's most powerful tools. Whether your poem rhymes or not, how it sounds when read aloud changes how it feels. In this revision lesson, you'll focus on how to hear your own poem more clearly and adjust it for rhythm, repetition, smoothness, and meter.

Start by reading your poem out loud. Slowly. Then again, faster. How does it move through your mouth and your ears? Where does it stumble? Where does it flow? Listen for awkward phrases or moments that feel flat or clunky. When something sounds "off," it often means a word is out of place or the rhythm is broken. That's your invitation to revise.

To review, poetry uses sound in many ways:
- **Alliteration** (repeating beginning consonant sounds)
- **Assonance** (repeating vowel sounds)
- **Consonance** (repeating consonant sounds throughout)
- **Onomatopoeia** (words that imitate sound)
- **Repetition** (repeating words or phrases for rhythm or emphasis)
- **Rhyme and meter** (intentional patterns of sound and syllables)

Even poems without rhyme or meter can still sound musical. Listen to the patterns in your own poem. Where do the sounds reinforce your message or emotion? Where do they get in the way?

Let's look at a student example for the Popping Popcorn Poem activity

First Draft:

By Shivaanti P., age 14

Rain drums

like fingers on an old tin roof

whispers soft

like secrets from long ago

Leaves rattle

like brittle bones in wind

puddles splash

like laughter from a time I know

Thunder hums

a tired, distant song

raindrops chatter

like echoes on glass

The earth drinks deep

with thirsty sighs

Then

Silence falls

like memories that pass.

Teacher suggestions: I like the simile structure and the ending! I would suggest you add the "like" in the second lines of stanzas 5 & 7. Without it, your meter changes and they clunk.

Revised Version:

Rain drums

like fingers on an old tin roof

whispers soft

like secrets from long ago

Leaves rattle

like brittle bones in wind

puddles splash

like laughter from a time I know

Thunder hums

like a tired, distant song

raindrops chatter

like echoes on glass

> The earth drinks deep
>
> like thirsty sighs
>
> Then
>
> Silence falls
>
> like memories that pass.

The subtle change helps the poem flow and makes the ending more powerful.

During revision, try experimenting with:

Swapping flat words for ones with more sonic texture ("moves" can become "rushes" or "worries")

- Shortening or lengthening lines to create a more musical rhythm
- Repeating a key word or sound for effect
- Reading out loud and changing any word or phrase that doesn't sound right

If you're not sure where to start, try highlighting 2–3 lines that sound dull or awkward. Pick one and write three new versions using different sounds, word combinations, or line lengths. Choose the one that feels the most alive.

Remember, poetry was meant to be heard. The best way to revise sound is to listen—really listen—to your poem. The human ear is a great editor. Trust it.

Lesson 6 Activity

Purpose of the Activity:

This activity guides students through a focused revision process that emphasizes how a poem *sounds* when read aloud. Students revise for rhythm, flow, and musicality—enhancing their poem with sound tools like alliteration, repetition, and line variation. Students should also look at structure if that helps with sound quality. The goal is to help students trust their ear and recognize that poetry is meant to be heard, not just read.

Guided Learning:

1. **Choose a poem (or more) from Lesson 5.**

    Students select 1–3 poems written during the previous lesson. If one activity felt more successful or enjoyable, encourage students to start there.

2. **Read each poem aloud—twice.**

    First, read *slowly* to hear how each word and line moves. Then, read *quickly* to feel the poem's natural rhythm. Students should mark (underline, star, or circle) any spot that feels awkward, choppy, or too flat.

3. **Ask revision questions.**

    Prompt students to reflect on specific lines:
    - Where does my poem flow smoothly?
    - Where does it sound too plain, too long, or too jumpy?
    - Can I add **repetition**, **alliteration**, or a more vivid sound?

4. **Revise one line at a time.**

    For each marked spot, students try replacing or rearranging a word or phrase to improve the sound. They can:
    - Swap in a word with a stronger sound
    - Add a repeated word or phrase
    - Adjust the length or rhythm of a line
    - Add alliteration or onomatopoeia to sharpen tone
    - Revise the structure to strengthen sounds by changing

line breaks or stanzas
5. **Test and compare.**
Once changes are made, students read the revised version aloud. Ask: *Does it sound better? More like what I wanted to say or feel?* Encourage students to listen for flow and musicality more than perfection.
6. **Optional: Share with a partner or family member**
If possible, students can share their revised poem with someone else. That person should respond to two questions in the activity.

Scoring Options:
Traditional Grading: Use the "Poem Revision" Rubric found in Appendix A. Review their poem revisions as a group on one rubric. This activity is worth 25 points.
Benchmark Grading: This activity is worth 25 points. Award all the points if they reflect on and revise at least one poem.

Choose one, two, or three of your poems in this unit to revise. (If you really didn't like an activity, it's okay to set it aside for now. We will revisit it at the end of the course).
As you look at the poems from Lesson 5, consider the following questions:

- Where does your poem flow smoothly?
- Where does it sound awkward or flat?
- Can you add alliteration, repetition, or a new rhythm?

How to Revise
Step 1: Read your poem out loud twice—once slowly, once quickly. Mark any places where it stumbles or doesn't have the rhythm that matches the rest of the poem.

Step 2: Try swapping/replacing one word or phrase in each of those places to improve flow or enhance sound.

Optional: The revision process works best with a partner–a parent, sibling, or friend. Have them read your poem and ask them:
- Is there anywhere that the poem doesn't "sound" right?
- Are there any places I could change the structure to help the rhythm or meter of the poem?

UNIT 4: WORD CHOICE

In this unit, you'll explore how choosing the right word can make a big difference in your poem's tone, mood, and meaning. You'll experiment with words, play with exaggeration and understatement, and even bend the rules of grammar to make your writing more poetic. You'll also learn how to choose vivid nouns and verbs, explore unusual pairings, and build deeper meaning through puns, idioms, and syntax. Poetry is about saying a lot with a little—and in this unit, you'll practice making every word count.

Unit Objective:

Students will develop their ability to select strong, specific, and meaningful words in their poetry. They will explore how subtle differences in word choice affect tone, clarity, and emotional impact, and they will learn to revise for sharper, more deliberate language.

Unit Overview:

This unit focuses on the weight that each word carries in a poem. With limited space and maximum impact, poets must choose words that do more than just describe—they must evoke, suggest, surprise, and resonate. Students will learn how to replace vague or overused words with those that are more vivid, precise, or emotionally charged. Through guided activities, they'll experiment with rewriting for stronger verbs, more descriptive nouns, and language that better fits the tone of their work. By the end of this unit, students will be able to revise their poetry to say more with less—and to say it more powerfully.

Lesson 7: Word Choice

Objective:

Students will learn how to make their poems stronger by choosing more precise, vivid, and emotionally accurate words. They will experiment with tone, explore how word choice reveals voice, and practice crafting lines that express more with fewer, more deliberate words.

Overview:

This lesson helps students recognize that every word in a poem carries weight. Whether a poem is playful or serious, the words a poet selects shape how the reader feels, imagines, and interprets the piece. Students will learn how to spot vague or weak words and replace them with stronger options that better match their message or mood. Through writing exercises and short poem drafts, they will explore tone, voice, and emotional impact—all through the lens of vocabulary.

Content Review:

Before beginning this lesson, review how structure and sound help shape the reader's experience of a poem. Remind students that in previous lessons, they made decisions about *how* their poems looked and sounded. Now, they'll focus on *what* their words are doing. Revisit a line from one of their earlier poems and ask: *Does this word show us something or just fill space? Could it be stronger, more precise, or more emotional?*

Teaching Notes:

- **Begin with examples.** Share a basic sentence (e.g., "The dog ran down the street") and ask students to brainstorm stronger versions. What happens if we replace "ran" with "bounded," "lurched," or "snuck"? This exercise immediately shows how word choice affects tone and image.
- **Highlight tone shifts.** When students rewrite a scene with different moods, encourage them to *read aloud* and listen

for how their word choices shape feeling. Ask: *Which version sounds more curious? Which one feels sad or angry?*
- **Encourage creativity over complexity.** Make it clear that "strong word choice" doesn't mean using fancy or unusual words—it means choosing *the right words* for the emotion and image they want to create.
- **Celebrate voice.** Word choice isn't just about description—it's about personality. Encourage students to let their own voice shine through, whether it's dramatic, sarcastic, dreamy, or intense.

Word Choice

Poetry, in many ways, comes down to saying something unique in very few words. How does a poet do this? There are several elements that can help you choose the best words.

The English language is full of fun things you can do with words. There are basic parts of speech, such as nouns, verbs, adjectives, and adverbs. In poetry, you don't need to stick to the rules of the sentence. You can make a verb the actor in a poem ("Jump came to me one night and said"). An adjective can be a nonsense word that modifies a noun. Your imagination is the limit!

Word Meanings

When picking words, you want to pay attention to the connotative meaning of words. The **connotation** of a word is the meaning associated with a word beyond just the definition of the word. You can say "quiet" or you can say "silent" and they are synonyms (words that can be substituted for one another because they have a closely related meaning). But synonyms do not have the *same* meaning. That's where connotation comes in—"quiet" could mean not talking, while "silent" could imply deliberately refraining from talking: close, but quite different. And sometimes words have emotional feelings attached to them. For instance, calling someone a "fat cow" is very different than saying that they are "obese." The first one is mean, while the second is not.

There are also special words that you can use in fun ways in your poems.

Homophones are words that sound the same but are spelled differently and have different meanings (flour/flower, or to/too/two).

Homonyms are words that sound the same *and* have the same spelling but mean different things: bear (the animal) and bear (carry) or tire (for a car) and tire (in need a of nap). Technically, these are a special type of homophones.

Heteronyms are words that are spelled the same, but they have different pronunciations and meanings. Examples: desert (an arid place) and desert (leave). Lead (a metal) and lead (to guide someone). Minute (amount of time) or minute (small).

For some reason, in common English, a lot of people call all the words above "homonyms." This isn't technically correct, but a lot of people do it, probably because it is easy to remember that synonyms are different words but mean the same thing, while "homonyms" sound the same but mean different things—remembering these two as opposites makes sense to a lot of people. It's okay if you also fall into that habit, but it is good to know that it's a common misunderstanding! The poem below lists "homonyms" in its title, but it uses all of them.

a little use of homonyms never hurt anyone
By Sae Sun James

i will love you always
and i'll love you in all ways
love you past what's allowed
despite what my past cries aloud

i believe i've lost control altogether
because you've captured my mind
my heart
and soul all together
you have the steering wheel
the pedal
the brake
captivating
wonderful
and the power to break

Word Exaggerations

Some figurative language is all about playing with words and the relationship between them. This collection of tools creates meaning by the way the words interact: creating a connection, a humorous idea, or a picture through the combination.

Hyperbole and Understatements

Hyperbole and **Understatements** are exaggerations for dramatic effect. Hyperbole goes larger than what is true—a girl is more beautiful than ALL the stars in the sky. Emily Dickinson even wrote a poem about hyperbole:

'Tis whiter than an Indian Pipe --
'Tis dimmer than a Lace --
No stature has it, like a Fog
When you approach the place --
Nor any voice imply it here
Or intimate it there
A spirit -- how doth it accost --
What function hat the Air?
This limitless Hyperbole
Each one of us shall be --

'Tis Drama -- if Hypothesis
It be not Tragedy --

Understatement goes the other way—it underemphasizes something big for dramatic effect. Here, Robert Frost says that the two things he compares "will suffice" for the destruction of the world:

Fire and Ice
Some say the world will end in fire,
Some say in ice.
From what I've tasted of desire
I hold with those who favor fire.
But if it had to perish twice,
I think I know enough of hate
To say that for destruction ice
Is also great
And would suffice.

Idiom

An **idiom** is a group of words that has a meaning that can't be understood from the ordinary meanings of the words in it. Often, we would refer to it as "an expression" and we know that the phrase isn't meant to be taken literally or seriously. Idioms are particularly hard for people who learn English as a second language to grasp, and other languages have their own sayings that would be equally hard for us to understand.

I'm so tired. I have to hit the hay.
With the weather, the game is up in the air.
When he stole my girlfriend, he stabbed me in the back.
That cost an arm and a leg.
I'm all ears.

Example:
I tell you that, I'll never look you in the face again: but those that understood him smiled at one another and shook their heads; but, for mine own part, it was Greek to me.
—*Julius Caesar*, William Shakespeare

Pun

A pun is a play on words that uses a word that sounds like another or a word that has different possible meanings to make a joke.

The tallest building in town is the library: it has thousands of stories.

Example:
Alice: "You see the earth takes twenty-four hours to turn round on its axis—"
"Talking of axes," said the Duchess, "chop off her head!"
—*Alice in Wonderland*, Lewis Carroll

Word Structures

Poetic Diction references the particular kind of language and complex arrangement of words that a poet uses. Instead of saying "I love you" perhaps a poet would say, as Elizabeth Barrett Browning did in "Sonnet 43":

> How do I love thee? Let me count the ways.
> I love thee to the depth and breadth and height
> My soul can reach, when feeling out of sight
> For the ends of being and ideal grace.
> I love thee to the level of every day's
> Most quiet need, by sun and candle-light.
> I love thee freely, as men strive for right.

I love thee purely, as they turn from praise.
I love thee with the passion put to use
In my old griefs, and with my childhood's faith.
I love thee with a love I seemed to lose
With my lost saints. I love thee with the breath,
Smiles, tears, of all my life; and, if God choose,
I shall but love thee better after death.

In poetry, there is a language of decorum that must be selected and adapted from depending on what the purpose of the poetry calls for. An ode, like the one above, sometimes uses specialized diction which often includes archaic language like "thee" and "thine." Often poetic diction is considered "too fancy" and then becomes clunky (like saying "feathered breed" instead of "birds"). This is a special kind of writing, and if you use words like this, your poems will sound very formal. That can be fun to write sometimes, but isn't intended for every poem, and can sometimes feel somewhat out-of-date. If you use this, often it should be used in a comical way (like an "ode" to smelly socks or something).

Syntax simply means word order. While poetic diction is about the kinds of words you use, syntax is about the order you place them in. Most of your poetry should be in proper order (like in a sentence). But every once in a while, structuring words in unusual way can make a line pop—so use it carefully! Yoda from Star Wars uses syntax in an unusual way—instead of saying a sentence in the right order, he says "Try not. Do or do not. There is no try." That's playing with syntax. A poet can do the same thing to create a new meaning, or to make the reader thing, or to help them pay attention to a certain word or to keep a rhythm or rhyme scheme consistent. For example, in the balcony scene of Romeo and Juliet, Shakespeare had Romeo say:

What light through yonder window breaks?
It is the east, and Juliet is the sun.

Why not say "What is that light in the window over there?" Changing the order makes us pay attention to the words "light" and "breaks"—it highlights his metaphor of Juliet being the light of his life (the name Juliet actually means "light"), and the idea of breaking highlights how he feels in his heart about loving the daughter of his enemy. All that from just changing word order!

A Paradox is a statement or situation containing what at first glance appear to be contradictory or incompatible ideas, but on closer inspection it may be true. In this poem, Robert Frost says that green is gold and a leaf is a flower...which seems untrue, until you think about a tree in spring:

Nothing Gold Can Stay

Nature's first green is gold,
Her hardest hue to hold.
Her early leaf's a flower;
But only so an hour.
Then leaf subsides to leaf.
So Eden sank to grief,
So dawn goes down to day.
Nothing gold can stay.

Parallelism is using the same word structure for more than one phrase repeatedly. This is similar to repetition, which we learned about last week, but this refers more to the words used (or, to say it a different way: parallelism creates repetition). It could be in the same line, or across several lines. The poem above by Elizabeth Barrett Browning uses "I love thee" to start most of her lines. Gwendolyn Brooks uses the word "we" in an unusual parallel way here:

We Real Cool

We real cool. We
Left school. We

Lurk late. We
Strike straight. We

Sing sin. We
Thin gin. We

Jazz June. We
Die soon.

Parallelism can also work through structure. Notice here in the 24th Psalm of David, there is a parallelism in alternating stanzas—stanza 1 and stanza 3 are parallel, and stanza 2 and 4 are parallel, with only a few changes that highlights a different quality of God.

Lift up your heads, you gates;
  be lifted up, you ancient doors,
  that the King of glory may come in.

Who is this King of glory?
  The LORD strong and mighty,
  the LORD mighty in battle.

Lift up your heads, you gates;
  lift them up, you ancient doors,
  that the King of glory may come in.

Who is he, this King of glory?
  The LORD Almighty—

he is the King of glory.

Lesson 7 Activity A: Activity 1: Line-by-Line Poem

Purpose of the Activity:]
This scaffolded exercise helps students build a full poem while focusing intentionally on one poetic technique per line. By following line-by-line prompts—including literary devices, structural tools, and wordplay—students stretch their creativity and strengthen their control over craft. The end result is often surprising and layered, showing students how word choice, sound, and form work together to create a powerful poem.

Have the students complete the activity on their own use the guided learning together,

Guided Learning:

1. **Set the tone for experimentation.**

    Explain to students that this is a *guided experiment*. They'll be writing one line at a time using specific instructions—but the content and interpretation are up to them. Emphasize that the goal is not perfection, but creative play.

2. **Review vocabulary if needed.**

    Before beginning, quickly revisit or define key terms:
    - End-stopped line
    - Internal rhyme
    - Syntax
    - Hyperbole
    - Allusion
    - Assonance
    - Enjambment
    - Alliteration

    Encourage students to keep past notes or lesson pages nearby for reference.

3. **Write the poem one line at a time.**

    Read the directions aloud and have students pause to write

each line before moving to the next. The lines should be connected to an idea or theme (usually created by the first line or two).

4. **Encourage creative freedom.**
Let students know that they can add stanza breaks *anywhere* or write as one long stanza. Remind them that it's okay if the poem doesn't "make sense" at first—it's about form and discovery.

Scoring Options:
Traditional Grading: Use the "Poem First Draft" Rubric found in Appendix A. In the tools section, you can reference sound, structure, and word choice. This poem is worth 20 points.
Benchmark Grading: This poem is worth 20 points. Award 6 points for completing the poem and 1 point each for following the instructions in each line.

Follow the guidelines below and without deviation, trying your best to fulfill the requirements of each line before moving on to the next one. Just trust me here—you might come up with something pretty fantastic!!
You may add stanza breaks wherever you feel they fit best, or have no breaks at all. You may need last week's lesson to reference some of these words.

Line 1: Write a line that has a smell in it.
Line 2: Make a one-line, end-stopped statement about a city.
Line 3: Comment on the time of year, the season, or the weather.
Line 4: Use an internal rhyme.
Line 5: Use syntax in an unusual way.
Line 6: Write a line with hyperbole and color(s) in it.
Line 7: Finish a sentence that begins "Next year at this time…"
Line 8: Make an allusion to a book, movie, or artwork.
Line 9: Be sure this line assonance AND enjambs.
Line 10: Make this line a question.

Line 11: Alliterate at least three words in this line.
Line 12: Make this line shorter or longer than the previous one by five or more words.
Line 13: Write whatever you like!
Line 14: End with a word picture.

Lesson 7 Activity B: Nouns and Verbs Poem

Purpose of the Activity:
This activity challenges students to break free from cliché imagery by forcing them to combine unexpected nouns and verbs. By using random sources and focusing on surprising pairings, students learn to stretch their descriptive language, create more original metaphors, and bring freshness and unpredictability to their poetry. This builds creative risk-taking and strengthens word choice by encouraging bold, unusual combinations.

Have the students complete the activity on their own use the guided learning together,

Guided Learning:

1. **Find a source and gather words.**

    Have students choose a source—this could be a book, website, newspaper, or even a game manual. Instruct them to skim until they've found **15 nouns and 15 verbs**, skipping any linking verbs like *is, was, are,* or *were*. They should simply list the first ones they come across.

2. **Select and combine 4 noun–verb pairs.**

    From their list, students choose **four nouns** and **four verbs**, then mix and match them into **four interesting combinations**. Encourage them to **avoid the obvious** (e.g., *the bird flew*) and instead find pairings that surprise or intrigue (e.g., *the window wept* or *sunlight swallowed the bricks*). Verbs can be conjugated, and nouns pluralized, if needed.

3. **Write a poem using all four combinations.**

    Students draft a poem that includes **each of their four noun–verb pairs**. There is no required length or structure—only that the poem uses the combinations in ways that feel creative and poetic. It can be narrative, imagistic, surreal, or grounded in emotion.

Scoring Options:

Traditional Grading: Use the "Poem First Draft" Rubric found in Appendix A. In the tools section, you can reference sound, structure, and word choice. This poem is worth 20 points.

Benchmark Grading: This poem is worth 20 points. Award 4 points for completing the poem and 4 point each for the noun-verb combinations.

Often when we write poetry, we fall into the same ruts: birds soar, streams trickle, waves roll. For this activity, we will be breaking out of our boring ruts and creating some new combinations.

1. Go to the internet (or a book) and open it. Read the first thing you find and simply write down the first 15 nouns and verbs you come across. Skip any linking verbs (was, is, were, etc).
2. Choose 4 nouns and 4 verbs and combine them into pairs (you may change verb endings or make nouns plural).
3. Write a poem using those four combinations—the more unusual, the better!!

Example
By Bert Meyers
The rusty nail shrieked
 pulled from the place where it lived...
 Flowers burst from the walls.
 The boat, a huge altar, dissolves in the fog.
 Sunlight plays its flute in the treetops.
 Night's swept away like a broken glass.
 the fallen man curls around a wall like smoke...
 At noon an airplane, a hard drop of sweat, rolls down the sky's big forehead.
 The light drips like oil from an old machine.

Lesson 7 Activity C: Tone Shift Poem

Purpose of the Activity:
This activity helps students understand how tone—the emotional quality of a poem—is shaped by word choice, rhythm, and structure. By writing two poems about the *same event* with *two different tones*, students learn how even simple shifts in vocabulary or syntax can completely change a poem's emotional impact. This strengthens their ability to revise with intention and gives them greater control over the reader's experience.

Have the students complete the activity on their own use the guided learning together,

Guided Learning:
1. **Choose an event.**
   Have students select a simple action-based event from the list provided or create one of their own (e.g., *a door opening, a plate falling, a pencil breaking*). The event should include a clear noun and verb.
2. **Select a tone.**
   Students choose one tone for their first version of the poem. Look at the tone list together and discuss how tone influences word choice, rhythm, and punctuation.
3. **Write Poem A.**
   Students write their first poem about the event using words, phrases, and structure that match the chosen tone. Encourage them to focus on:
   - Verbs that reflect mood
   - Sensory details that evoke tone
   - Pacing and line breaks
4. **Choose a different tone.**
   Now students pick a **new tone** that contrasts with or shifts the mood of the first (e.g., from creepy to joyful, from frustrated to grateful).
5. **Write Poem B.**

Using the same event, students rewrite the poem in the new tone. Remind them they can completely change the wording, rhythm, and imagery—as long as the basic event remains the same.

6. **Compare and reflect.**

    Have students read both poems aloud and discuss:
    - What changed between versions?
    - Which word choices helped create the tone?
    - How did structure or rhythm support the mood?

7. **Optional partner feedback.**

    Students can share poems with a peer who guesses each poem's tone and offers one suggestion for clarifying mood through word choice.

Scoring Options:

Traditional Grading: Use the "Poem First Draft" Rubric found in Appendix A. In the tools section, you can reference sound, structure, and word choice. This poem is worth 20 points.

Benchmark Grading: This poem is worth 20 points. Award 10 points for each poem, making sure that they both have a different tone.

Step 1: Choose a simple event that includes a noun and an action. You can pick anything, but here are some ideas:

A door opening	A phone ringing
A pencil breaking	A woman shouting
A bird chirping	A baby crying
A squirrel running	A snake hiding
A plate falling	

Step 2: Now, pick a tone (tone is the mood of the poem) and write a poem about the event. Use one of these or come up with your own:

Angry	Joyful	Nervous	Curious
Sarcastic	Lonely	Playful	Formal

Excited	Creepy	Calm	Confused
Grateful	Dramatic	Suspicious	Embarrassed
Hopeful	Tired	Frustrated	Welcoming
Proud	Indifferent	Jealous	Peaceful
Scared	Awkward	Uneasy	

Step 3: Then write a SECOND poem with a DIFFERENT tone. Don't change the event, just the words. Think about:
- Verbs (tiptoed vs stomped)
- Nouns (glow vs glare)
- Adjectives (slick vs slimy)
- Sentence structure and rhythm

You ARE allowed to change the words and action, but the event you picked in Step #1 should be the same in both poems

Example:
Poem A (uneasy tone)
The knob jerked
As he wrenched it open..
He stormed in,
shoulders squared,
eyes squinting at the culprit.
No one spoke.

Poem B (welcoming tone)
The door squeaked
As he quietly opened it.
He peeked in,
grinned wide,
arms full of books.
We waved him in.

Lesson 8: Revisions with Word Choice

Objective:

Students will revise one or more poems with a focus on improving word choice. They will identify vague, flat, or overly familiar language and experiment with replacing it using more specific, vivid, and emotionally resonant words.

Overview:

In this lesson, students learn that strong poems rely on precision. Even small changes in language can elevate the tone, clarify the message, and deepen the emotional impact. Students will practice identifying weaker lines in their drafts and revising them with intention—replacing bland or overused words with stronger verbs, specific nouns, or tone-appropriate adjectives. Through guided reflection and revision, they'll learn to say more with less and use words that truly matter.

Content Review:

Before beginning this lesson, review the idea that every word in a poem carries weight. Revisit examples from Lesson 7 and ask:

- What's the difference between "The day was good" and "The sun slipped through the grass"?
- How can a single word (like *shattered* or *flickered*) shift the tone of a whole stanza?

Reinforce that good poems aren't filled with fancy vocabulary—they're built on deliberate word choices that match the purpose and tone of the poem.

Teaching Notes:

- **Model how to spot weak words.** Use a sample line and underline words like *good, bad, really, very,* or *thing*. Brainstorm stronger alternatives with students and discuss how each choice affects tone.
- **Encourage revision one line at a time.** Students don't need to rewrite the entire poem. Focus on 1–3 lines that feel unclear, flat, or generic.

- **Offer concrete tools.** Provide students with revision strategies such as:
    - Replace weak verbs with specific actions
    - Swap out abstract nouns with sensory or visual nouns
    - Match adjectives to tone and emotion

Every word in a poem has a job. Unlike stories or essays, poems don't have space for filler words. That's why revising for word choice is one of the most important steps in making your poem stronger. The words you choose shape your poem's voice, tone, rhythm, and impact. In this lesson, we'll work on sharpening your word choices so that every line pulls its weight.

When revising, ask yourself: Are these the most specific, surprising, or powerful words I can use? Are there any vague or overused words that don't help the poem shine? Words like "nice," "good," "very," or "a lot" might work in casual writing, but they don't belong in poetry unless they're used deliberately for contrast or tone.

Let's look at a student example.

First Draft:

[Line-by-line Poem]

By Aaron C., Age 17

Bamboozled brains berated by branding banes.

Brown brown brown, hair, eyes, and warmth all around.

Spring spills through the woods stomping out ice, leaving puddles in its wake

A clown with a frown before the crown is a sure way to go down.

Easy too is this, dyslexic I am so

Poems are a fountain from the mind

Once I had realized I was in town I started to wander around

So many of us are a doubting Thomas

The car was a bullet along the track

The burial mound had many mourning in misery

The solitary sound eerily echoed like a single shot from a vengeful bullet

Why, if we can see, we look to hear?

Black strokes on the core, smoldering wet bark, shattered limbs like fallen soldiers in the mud

[Note: Aaron said that he hated this poem, and the instructor suggested pulling out the best phrases and creating a more meaningful piece out of what he did like using specific words to evoke emotions.]

Revised Version:

Spring spills through the night woods.

A solitary sound eerily echoes

like a single shot from a vengeful bullet.

In a crowd of raindrops the tallest of oaks falls,

black strokes on the core, smoldering wet bark and shattered limbs,

like fallen soldiers in the mud.

The whole forest is undone.

Now, the words feel more deliberate and specific. The

addition of "Night woods" gives a specific setting and the final line lends weight to the idea of taking down a forest, which was lost in the original poem.

It also helps to ask: What tone am I going for? Gentle? Angry? Dreamy? Do the words in the poem match that tone? A calm poem probably shouldn't be full of jagged, harsh-sounding words. A wild, energetic poem shouldn't rely on soft, flat ones.

During revision, play around. Try different synonyms. Don't forget that sometimes the best word is the simplest one. Precision isn't about sounding smart—it's about choosing the word that fits the moment best. When the word is right, it disappears into the meaning.

Make every line count. Replace vague or bland words with strong, specific ones. Choose language that reflects the tone and purpose of your poem. A small change in word choice can completely transform a poem.

Lesson 8 Activity

Purpose of the Activity:
This activity helps students apply revision strategies specifically focused on word choice. By identifying weak or vague lines in their own poems and experimenting with sharper alternatives, students learn how precise language can elevate meaning, tone, and imagery. The exercise also reinforces that revision is not about fixing "mistakes," but about making purposeful choices that reflect the poet's voice and intent.

Have the student write their own outline, or complete the guided learning below together.

Guided Learning: During the Activity: Support with Structure

1. **Choose one or more poems from Lesson 7.**
   Students select a poem they wrote during the Word Choice lesson. Remind them they don't need to revise everything—just the parts that could be clearer or more vivid.

2. **Identify the heart of the poem.**
   Have students write one sentence that explains what their poem is really about (emotion, idea, or moment). This will help them revise with that focus in mind.

3. **Highlight strong and weak lines.**
   Students read their poem aloud and:
   - Star one line they feel is working well (specific, powerful, or emotional)
   - Underline one line that feels vague, plain, or off-tone

4. **Revise the weak line three ways.**
   Using different techniques (strong verbs, vivid nouns, sensory words, tone-matching adjectives), students write three new versions of their underlined line. This gives them options to compare and builds creative flexibility.

5. **Choose the strongest version.**
   After reading all three out loud, students pick the version that best matches their intent and tone. They then rewrite

the poem with the new line.
6. **Optional partner reflection.**
   Students can trade poems with a partner and ask:
   - Which word or image stands out the most?
   - Is there a word or line that could be more specific or poetic?

Scoring Options:
Traditional Grading: Use the "Poem Revision" Rubric found in Appendix A. Review their poem revisions as a group on one rubric. This activity is worth 25 points.
Benchmark Grading: This activity is worth 25 points. Award all the points if they reflect on and revise at least one poem.

Choose one, two, or three of your poems from this unit to revise. To revise your own word choice, start by circling three words in your poem that feel too plain or general. Try replacing them with more descriptive, sensory, or surprising alternatives. You might use:
- Strong verbs (e.g., "run" → "sprint," "fly" → "dart")
- Unusual adjectives (e.g., "blue" → "bruised," "loud" → "howling")
- Specific nouns (e.g., "bird" → "sparrow," "tree" → "sycamore")

You don't need fancy vocabulary—just precise words that fit the voice of your poem.

Optional: The revision process works best with a partner–a parent, sibling, or friend. Have them read your poem and ask them:
- What would you say the tone of the poem is, and do the words match it?
- What word or line do you think I could make more specific to help make this tone clear?

UNIT 5: IMAGERY

In this unit, you'll learn how to use images to express emotion, memory, and meaning without directly saying how you feel. You'll explore tools like similes, metaphors, and personification to create pictures with words. You'll also discover how poets use allusions, paradox, and symbolism to add deeper layers to their poems. Whether you're describing a moment from your life or imagining a completely new one, imagery helps your reader see, feel, and experience your ideas.

Unit Objective:

Students will develop their ability to use descriptive, sensory language to create vivid images and emotions in poetry. They will practice writing with figurative language, metaphor, and concrete detail to help readers *see, hear, feel,* and *experience* what the poem expresses.

Unit Overview:

This unit focuses on one of poetry's most essential elements: imagery. Strong poems don't just tell the reader what to feel—they create a scene, a sound, a smell, a moment the reader can step into. Students will learn how to move beyond abstract ideas by grounding their writing in the five senses and by using figurative language like similes and metaphors. They'll also explore conceptual imagery, which uses concrete pictures to represent emotions or ideas. By the end of the unit, students will know how to make their poetry more immersive, emotionally rich, and memorable.

Lesson 9: Imagery

Objective:
Students will learn how to use imagery to strengthen the emotional and visual impact of their poetry. They will practice describing scenes, emotions, and ideas using the five senses and figurative language such as similes and metaphors.

Overview:
This lesson introduces students to imagery as one of the most powerful tools in poetry. Instead of telling the reader how to feel, students will learn to show it—through sensory details and concrete images. They will explore both direct imagery (describing what something looks, smells, or feels like) and conceptual imagery (using metaphor or symbol to represent abstract ideas). The goal is to help students move from general statements to vivid, memorable scenes and sensations.

Content Review:
Before beginning this lesson, review the difference between abstract and concrete language. Ask students to brainstorm a few examples of each. For example:

- Abstract: love, fear, happiness, regret
- Concrete: cold rain, cracked pavement, a trembling hand

Revisit how previous lessons on word choice and tone can now work together with imagery. Remind students that they've already been using some sensory detail—but in this lesson, they'll focus on doing it deliberately.

Teaching Notes:

- **Start with an example.** Read a professional poem that uses strong sensory detail (any of the poems in this lesson will work well for an introduction). Ask students what they can see, hear, or feel in the poem.
- **Introduce the five senses + figurative language.** Explain that strong imagery combines concrete details with figurative comparisons. Similes and metaphors let us

- describe the *feeling* of an idea—not just what it looks like.
- **Encourage grounding in real experience.** Sensory writing is often strongest when it comes from memory or direct observation. Let students close their eyes and picture a place or moment before writing.
- **Allow for emotional interpretation.** Some students may want to write about intense emotions (e.g., loneliness, anxiety). Offer examples that model how those feelings can be shown through concrete images rather than directly stated.
- **Focus on precision.** Good imagery doesn't mean stuffing the poem with adjectives. Guide students to choose specific nouns and verbs first, then refine with metaphor or sensory detail.

Images are key to poems—part of a good poem is creating a picture of an abstract idea. The best poems are the ones rooted in concrete ideas to express the things that are indescribable. It is the unique way that a poem captures an emotion that gives it power.

So how do we do this? There are several techniques we can use in our writing to effectively create images or concrete ideas. One way to create images is through figurative language, and another is through sensory and symbolic descriptions Both ways help the reader SEE an idea using concrete, specific words.

Figurative Language

Figurative language is when a writer uses words or expressions in a creative way to suggest meaning beyond their literal definition. We discussed word exaggerations in the "Word Choice" lesson–this is a type of figurative language that uses words to create humor. In this lesson, we are focusing on language that creates a picture in the reader's mind. Poets often use figurative language to say something in a more imaginative or powerful way. Instead of stating things directly, they use comparisons, personifications, or references to help readers experience an idea more deeply by picturing it. Figurative language isn't meant to be taken literally—it helps paint a picture, show emotion, or reveal meaning in a fresh way.

Metaphors and Similes

Similes and metaphors are comparisons that the poet makes between two things. A simile uses "like" or "as" ("my love is like a red, red rose") and a metaphor does not ("It is the east and Juliet is the sun"). Often a poet uses similes and metaphors to say something common, which makes it both unique and gives it a depth that perhaps the reader has not thought of before. An extended metaphor is a comparison that carries throughout the poem:

Metaphors

A **metaphor** is a comparison between two items or phenomena that normally would not be connected using the words is or was.

My dad is an angry volcano.
We were couch potatoes all weekend.

Examples:
All the world's a stage / And all the men and women merely, players.
—As You Like It, William Shakespeare

All religions, arts and sciences are branches of the same tree.
—Albert Einstein

The sun in the west was a drop of burning gold that slid near and nearer the sill of the world. —Lord of the Flies, William Golding

Similes

Like a metaphor, a **simile** is a comparison between two items or phenomena that normally would not be connected but unlike a metaphor, a simile makes the comparison using the words *like* or *as:* As brave as a lion, as busy as a bee, as clear as mud.

Examples:
Life is like a box of chocolates. —Forrest Gump

She entered with ungainly struggle like some huge awkward chicken, torn, squawking, out of its coop.
—The Adventure of the Three Gables, Sir Arthur Conan Doyle

The water made a sound like kittens lapping.
—The Yearling, Marjorie Kinnan Rawlings

Conceptual Figurative Language

This collection of figurative language tools goes beyond the meaning of the words to create a larger understanding of an idea. Sometimes these ideas are repeated throughout a work to add to a theme.

Personification

Personification is giving a personality to inanimate objects like the sun or the dawn. Throughout the Odyssey, Homer calls the dawn "rosy-fingered" or "she." Emily Dickinson did this a lot in her poetry as well:
"Hope" is the thing with feathers --
That perches in the soul --
And sings the tune without the words --

And never stops -- at all –

Adjectives and adverbs can also be used to give human feelings to objects: "mischievous wind" or "laughing brook." This can be a powerful tool, but it can also lead to trite clichés so try to come up with an idea that hasn't been overdone.

Allusions

Allusions are implicit references to other works of literature, art, films, people, or events. You might say, "I don't mind airport security because I don't want another 9/11 to happen" and I would understand that you are referring to the terrorist attacks that occurred using planes on September 11, 2001. Poets do the same thing. This gives a work depth and allows the poet to create a shared experience with the reader.

Sometimes this is done by referring to a famous work. How do you understand these? Increase your library of reader-knowledge! The most famous works used in literary allusions are the Bible and Shakespeare. You don't need to read everything but understanding common references will help you. For example, you can refer to your childhood as an "Eden"—most people will understand that you felt your childhood was perfect. The Homonyms activity from last week included a poem that started "to alter or to altar" which is an allusion to Hamlet's famous "to be or not to be" speech by Shakespeare.

Sometimes allusions are to events current to the writer. A reference to 9/11 in a poem would be an example of this. Or the author could refer to himself or another person. Shakespeare plays with the word "Will" (his first name) all the time, and John Donne uses his name in references to things being "done" or "undone." Here is the first stanza of Donne's poem "Hymn to God the Father." Substitute Donne's name in every time you see the word "done" and notice how much more impact (and double meaning) the poem has:

Wilt Thou forgive that sin where I begun,
   Which was my sin, though it were done before?
Wilt Thou forgive that sin, through which I run,
   And do run still, though still I do deplore?
     When Thou hast done, Thou hast not done,
        For I have more.

Paradox

A **paradox** is a statement that seems silly or contradicts itself and reveals a truth. "I must be cruel only to be kind," says Hamlet. Cruel and kind contradict one another. In *Animal Farm* by George Orwell, there's a rule that "All animals are equal, but some are more equal than others." *A Tale of Two Cities* by Charles Dickens starts, "It was the best of times, it was the worst of times." There are several proverbs or sayings that you've probably heard that are paradoxes when you think about it. Less is more. The enemy of my enemy is my friend. Failure leads to success.

Oxymoron

An **oxymoron** is a figure of speech that refers to a set of contradictory words. It may seem similar to a paradox, but a paradox is a statement or argument that seems to be contradictory or go against *common sense*, while an oxymoron is a group of words that are almost exact opposites of each other that create a new meaning.

Some oxymorons are phrases we use all the time: original copies, liquid gas, virtual reality, paid volunteers, old news, seriously funny. Some other examples are a love-hate relationship, absolutely unsure, or deafening silence.

Example:
Why, then, O brawling love! O loving hate!
O anything, of nothing first create!

O heavy lightness! Serious vanity!
Misshapen chaos of well-seeming forms!
Feather of lead, bright smoke, cold fire, sick health!
—Romeo and Juliet, William Shakespeare

Creating Images

Images are like word snapshots: they draw a picture of a moment in time for your reader to experience. They are usually used to connect our outer and inner worlds: a sad person would see a desolate landscape, and a content person might focus on the lazy way the bees buzz around the flowers. We can do this by making word pictures, using our senses, or letting objects stand in for ideas.

Images (Word Pictures)

Images are a little bit like metaphors, but they are not a direct comparison. A metaphor would say "In the deep lake of my soul sadness sits" (comparing your soul to a lake). An image would simply present the lake, "The blue waters fall into darkness" (there is no mention of the soul, but sadness is still portrayed). When the reader is presented with the image, they understand the emotion that the speaker feels.

The Meadow Mouse
By Theodore Roethke
1
In a shoe box stuffed in an old nylon stocking
Sleeps the baby mouse I found in the meadow,
Where he trembled and shook beneath a stick
Till I caught him up by the tail and brought him in,
Cradled in my hand,
A little quaker, the whole body of him trembling,
His absurd whiskers sticking out like a cartoon-mouse,

His feet like small leaves,
Little lizard-feet,
Whitish and spread wide when he tried to struggle away,
Wriggling like a minuscule puppy.

Now he's eaten his three kinds of cheese and drunk from his
bottle-cap watering-trough--
So much he just lies in one corner,
His tail curled under him, his belly big
As his head; his bat-like ears
Twitching, tilting toward the least sound.

Do I imagine he no longer trembles
When I come close to him?
He seems no longer to tremble.

2
But this morning the shoe-box house on the back porch is empty.
Where has he gone, my meadow mouse,
My thumb of a child that nuzzled in my palm? --
To run under the hawk's wing,
Under the eye of the great owl watching from the elm-tree,
To live by courtesy of the shrike, the snake, the tom-cat.

I think of the nestling fallen into the deep grass,
The turtle gasping in the dusty rubble of the highway,
The paralytic stunned in the tub, and the water rising,--
All things innocent, hapless, forsaken.

Sensory Details

Sensory details are descriptive details that utilize each of your five senses (often in combination) to describe something. Instead of just telling your reader what happened, help them feel like they were there. Ask yourself: *What did it look like? Sound like? Smell like? Feel like? Taste like?* These are called sensory **details**, and they make your writing vivid and memorable. A single well-chosen sensory detail—like "the sticky sweetness of melted popsicle on my fingers"—can say more than a whole paragraph of explanation.

Read this poem by Imatiaz Dharker, about a water line breaking during a drought and notice how she uses sight, sound, touch, and taste to create an image of a community.

Blessing
By Imatiaz Dharker

The skin cracks like a pod.
There never is enough water.

Imagine the drip of it,
the small splash, echo
in a tin mug,
the voice of a kindly god.

Sometimes, the sudden rush
of fortune. The municipal pipe bursts,
silver crashes to the ground
and the flow has found
a roar of tongues. From the huts,
a congregation: every man woman
child for streets around
butts in, with pots,
brass, copper, aluminium,
plastic buckets,
frantic hands,

and naked children

screaming in the liquid sun,
their highlights polished to perfection,
flashing light,
as the blessing sings
over their small bones.

Symbolism

Symbolism is using an object or work to represent an abstract idea. An action, person, place, word, or object can all have symbolic meaning. When you want to suggest a certain mood or emotion, you can use symbolism to hint at it, instead of expressing it blatantly. For example, think of the use of colors. Red often represents love or romance. Green represents spring and new beginnings. Black may represent night or death.

Some symbols are universal and are accepted as meaning certain things (spring=rebirth, bird=flying/freedom, lion=courage, rose=beauty). This can be helpful in writing poetry in two ways: first, you can reference a symbol and assume your audience will understand the emotion ("I became a lion and roared as I leapt"). Second, you can use those assumptions to shock or create comedy in a poem ("She is a rose that smells rotten").

But some symbols are specific to a story or work. In literature, we can analyze symbols that carry throughout the novel to point to larger ideas. In *The Scarlet Letter,* Hester Prynne is a Puritan who has to wear an "A" on her clothes as punishment. It symbolizes her sin for all to see. In *The Great Gastby,* the green light on the far side of the water symbolizes Gatsy's hopes and dreams for the future. In Edgar Allan Poe's poem "The Raven," the black bird symbolizes death and loss.

In this poem, the road becomes a symbol for traveling through life. Images are used to support this idea and the symbol of the untraveled road tells us how the speaker feels about the choices he has made in life.

The Road Not Taken
By Robert Frost

Two roads diverged in a yellow wood,
And sorry I could not travel both
And be one traveler, long I stood
And looked down one as far as I could
To where it bent in the undergrowth;

Then took the other, as just as fair,
And having perhaps the better claim
Because it was grassy and wanted wear,
Though as for that the passing there
Had worn them really about the same,

And both that morning equally lay
In leaves no step had trodden black.
Oh, I kept the first for another day!
Yet knowing how way leads on to way
I doubted if I should ever come back.

I shall be telling this with a sigh
Somewhere ages and ages hence:
Two roads diverged in a wood, and I,
I took the one less traveled by,
And that has made all the difference.

Lesson 9 Activity A: Afterimages Poem

Purpose of the Activity:
This activity guides students to transform a personal memory into a vivid, image-rich poem. By focusing on physical and sensory details—rather than summary or explanation—students learn how to evoke strong emotion through imagery. It encourages reflection, mindfulness, and concrete language while building confidence in using poetic tools to express real experiences.

Guided Learning:
1. **Brainstorm five experiences.**
   Have students list five moments from their life that felt physically or emotionally intense. These could be:
   - Small but vivid (e.g., falling off a bike, a thunderstorm, cleaning a messy room)
   - Big and personal (e.g., a funeral, getting in trouble, a big win or loss)

   Remind them that it doesn't have to be dramatic—it just needs to feel memorable in their body.

2. **Choose one moment to explore.**
   Ask students to select the experience that feels most vivid or meaningful. Encourage them to trust their instinct—the best poems often come from unexpected places.

3. **Use all five senses to recall the moment.**
   Before writing, have students close their eyes and "re-enter" the memory. Prompt them to think through:
   - What did you see?
   - What sounds do you remember?
   - What textures or physical feelings were present?
   - Were there smells or tastes?
   - What thoughts or emotions surprised you?

4. **Jot down sensory phrases.**
   Students should quickly list or sketch out as many descriptive phrases as possible—concrete details,

comparisons, fragments of memory. These don't have to be complete sentences yet.

5. **Write the poem.**

   Using their notes, students create a poem about the memory. It can be:
   - A retelling of the moment in real time
   - A reflection written from the future
   - A memory layered with dream or metaphor

   Encourage them to focus on images, sensory detail, and figurative language.

Scoring Options:

Traditional Grading: Use the "Poem First Draft" Rubric found in Appendix A. In the tools section, you can reference sound, structure, and word choice. This poem is worth 20 points.

Benchmark Grading: This poem is worth 20 points. Award 10 points for completing the poem, 5 points for sensory language, and 5 points for at least one image.

Create a poem looking back on an experience you had using mostly images. Here's how to do that:

1. Make a list of five intense physical experiences you have had. Include both everyday things (cleaning out the garage) and monumental events (getting in a car crash). If you get stuck, think of the times you went to bed physically exhausted or emotionally drained.
2. Choose one of these events that is especially vivid. This is what you will write your poem about.
3. Without writing, think about that experience. Put yourself back in that moment and use all your senses—what did you feel, touch, taste, hear, see, smell? When you are ready, jot down phrases of experience. Include as many details as you can.
4. Using the phrases and memories, write a poem about that experience. Pay special attention to thoughts or senses that

surprised you. You can simply describe the experience, or you can place yourself in another location remembering the experience.

Example
   After Apple-Picking
   By Robert Frost

My long two-pointed ladder's sticking through a tree
Toward heaven still,
And there's a barrel that I didn't fill
Beside it, and there may be two or three
Apples I didn't pick upon some bough.
But I am done with apple-picking now.
Essence of winter sleep is on the night,
The scent of apples: I am drowsing off.
I cannot rub the strangeness from my sight
I got from looking through a pane of glass
I skimmed this morning from the drinking trough
And held against the world of hoary grass.
It melted, and I let it fall and break.
But I was well
Upon my way to sleep before it fell,
And I could tell
What form my dreaming was about to take.
Magnified apples appear and disappear,
Stem end and blossom end,
And every fleck of russet showing clear.
My instep arch not only keeps the ache,
It keeps the pressure of a ladder-round.
I feel the ladder sway as the boughs bend.
And I keep hearing from the cellar bin
The rumbling sound
Of load on load of apples coming in.

For I have had too much
Of apple-picking: I am overtired
Of the great harvest I myself desired.
There were ten thousand thousand fruit to touch,
Cherish in hand, lift down, and not let fall.
For all
That struck the earth,
No matter if not bruised or spiked with stubble,
Went surely to the cider-apple heap
As of no worth.
One can see what will trouble
This sleep of mine, whatever sleep it is.
Were he not gone,
The woodchuck could say whether it's like his
Long sleep, as I describe its coming on,
Or just some human sleep.

Lesson 9 Activity B: Postcard Poem

Purpose of the Activity:
This activity helps students combine visual imagery, voice, and figurative language to create a poetic "postcard" from a real or imagined place. By stepping into a character's perspective and describing a setting as if it were a postcard image, students practice using metaphor, sensory detail, and concise structure to tell a story. It blends observation with imagination while reinforcing strong image-making and vivid verbs.

Guided Learning:
1. **Choose a location.**
   Have students select a place for their postcard poem. It can be somewhere they've visited, somewhere they've always wanted to go, or a famous landmark or natural setting. They should search for and select a photo of that location—one that could be featured on a postcard.
2. **Imagine the sender.**
   Next, students invent a character (not themselves!) who might be sending that postcard. Encourage them to think about:
   - Who is this person?
   - Why are they there?
   - What do they wish or hope for?
   - What are they feeling in that moment?
   - What do they want to say to or about the person they are "writing" (if anything)?

   This perspective gives the poem voice and personality.
3. **Describe the image and experience.**
   Students write a poem in the voice of that character, describing the setting as if painting a picture for the recipient. Remind them that this isn't a typical postcard note—it's a poetic message, so they should focus on sensory description, metaphor, and mood.

5. **Include key requirements.**
    Review the requirements and remind them to include two metaphors and lots of action verbs.

Optional follow-up: Have students attach or print the image they used and mount it beside their poem for display or sharing.

Scoring Options:

Traditional Grading: Use the "Poem First Draft" Rubric found in Appendix A. In the tools section, you can reference sound, structure, and word choice. This poem is worth 20 points.

Benchmark Grading: This poem is worth 20 points. Award 10 points for completing the poem, 4 points for describing the image, and 3 points each for the two metaphors.

We have all seen postcards—or sent them!—while on vacation. With this poem, you are going to send a visual "postcard" to someone else. But instead of writing just the words for the postcard, you are going to write the picture that could be on the postcard. Here is how to do this:

1. Pick a location. It can be somewhere you have been, or somewhere you would like to go.
2. Google pictures of that location, and pick one that might be on a postcard. It can have people in it—you are allowed to be a little nontraditional here!
3. Imagine a person (NOT you!!) who might send that postcard. What would they write? What story would they tell about that picture or that moment?
4. Write a postcard that your imagined person that would send. Remember that you need to include the description of the picture as well as the activity.
5. Include at least two metaphors.
6. Make your verbs alive (action words!).
7. Title your poem "Postcard from [Location]"

Lesson 9 Activity C: What The Object Knows Poem

Purpose of the Activity:
This activity develops students' creative voice and descriptive power by asking them to write a poem from the perspective of a common object. By personifying something everyday, students practice using imagery, sensory detail, and point of view to reveal meaning. This encourages imaginative thinking while reinforcing the use of concrete language and figurative tools.

Guided Learning:
1. **Choose an object.**
   Ask students to pick an ordinary object they know well—something small and everyday. Examples might include a pair of socks, a pencil case, a doormat, or a phone charger.
2. **Give it a voice and point of view.**
   Have students imagine:
   - Does the object see and hear everything?
   - What is its tone: Is it wise, sarcastic, lonely, proud, or confused?
   - Does it misunderstand the world, or know more than anyone else?

   Remind them: *This object has all five senses.* It can describe the world in unexpected ways.
3. **Write the poem.**
   Students write their poem from the object's point of view, using a sense of attitude or voice (sarcasm, melancholy, humor, etc.). If they get stuck, have them imagine an event that this object can observe or be part of.

Scoring Options:
Traditional Grading: Use the "Poem First Draft" Rubric found in Appendix A. In the tools section, you can reference sound, structure, and word choice. This poem is worth 20 points.

Benchmark Grading: This poem is worth 20 points. Award 10 points for completing the poem, 4 points for describing the image, and 3 points each for the two metaphors.

Write a poem from the perspective of an object. Choose something everyday and common–a coffeepot, a sock, a set of keys, a water bottle, a book, a phone case.
- Think about what this object would say if it could talk. Imagine that it has all five senses.
- What does the object see, hear, smell, taste, or touch? And what meaning does it give to those things?
- Your object can be wise (it knows and understands everything), or foolish (it senses but draws the wrong conclusions).

Mirror
By Sylvia Plath

I am silver and exact. I have no preconceptions.
Whatever I see I swallow immediately
Just as it is, unmisted by love or dislike.
I am not cruel, only truthful,
The eye of a little god, four-cornered.
Most of the time I meditate on the opposite wall.
It is pink, with speckles. I have looked at it so long
I think it is part of my heart. But it flickers.
Faces and darkness separate us over and over.
Now I am a lake. A woman bends over me,
Searching my reaches for what she really is.
Then she turns to those liars, the candles or the moon.
I see her back, and reflect it faithfully.
She rewards me with tears and an agitation of hands.
I am important to her. She comes and goes.
Each morning it is her face that replaces the darkness.

In me she has drowned a young girl, and in me an old woman
Rises toward her day after day, like a terrible fish.

A Navajo Blanket
By May Swenson

   Eye-dazzlers the Indians weave. Three colors
   are paths that pull you in, and pin you
   to the maze. Brightness makes your eyes jump,
   surveying the geometric field. Alight, and enter
   any of the gates—of Blue, of Red, of Black.
   Be calmed and hooded, a hawk brought down,
   glad to fasten to the forearm of a Chief.
   You can sleep at the center,
   attended by Sun that never fades, by Moon
   that cools. Then, slipping free of zigzag and hypnotic diamond,
find your way out
   by the spirit trail, a faint Green thread that
   secretly crosses the border, where your mind
   is rinsed and returned to you like a white cup.

Chair
By Eleanor Scorah

I am the chair that holds your bum,
and your clothes, and the other random crap
you throw on me.
I miss the days when I was just a chair.
Your behind is far warmer than the half-worn clothes
you dump on me.
I long for you to to settle on me once more,
to be what you wanted me to be,
to hold you and not your belongings.
I know you don't look at me that way any more,

I am only what you want me to be,
what you use me for.
I wrap your coat around me
and make do with the smell of you,
the residual heat of you.

Lesson 10: Revising Imagery

Objective:

Students will revise one or more poems with a focus on strengthening imagery. They will identify abstract or vague lines and replace them with specific, sensory language that brings the poem's subject, setting, or emotion into sharper focus.

Overview:

In this lesson, students move from writing with imagery to revising for it. They will ask: *Can the reader see this? Hear it? Feel it?* By identifying lines that are too general, abstract, or flat, students will practice using concrete details, figurative language, and sensory phrasing to heighten the emotional and visual impact of their work. The goal is to transform poems from simply stated ideas into fully felt experiences.

Content Review:

Before beginning, review the five senses and the concept of figurative language (metaphor, simile, personification). Ask:

- What's the difference between "It was a sad day" and "Rain slid down the windows like a slow apology"?
- How can imagery show the reader what you're feeling without ever naming the emotion?

Remind students that good imagery doesn't rely on fancy adjectives—it uses specific nouns, strong verbs, and sensory comparisons that make the poem *come alive*.

Teaching Notes:

- **Read aloud first.** Encourage students to read their poem out loud before revising. This helps them hear where details feel strong and where the poem loses energy or clarity.
- **Highlight abstract lines.** Have students underline or highlight one or two lines that feel vague, overly general, or emotional without being descriptive (e.g., "I was sad," "It was perfect," "Everything was quiet").
- **Replace with image-based details.** Prompt students to

rewrite those lines by focusing on *what the emotion or idea looks/sounds/feels like.* Challenge them to use a metaphor, sensory details, or a concrete image.
- **Optional partner feedback.** Students may work in pairs to identify the strongest image in each other's poems and suggest one line that could benefit from more detail or specificity.
- **Focus on small wins.** Let students know they don't need to revise every line. If they can sharpen just one or two key images, their entire poem may become more powerful.

Imagery is one of the most powerful tools a poet can use. It brings your poem to life by helping your reader see, hear, feel, taste, or smell what you're describing. Rather than telling your reader what to feel, imagery invites them into an experience. In this lesson, we'll focus on how to revise your poem to include stronger, clearer images that reveal emotions and meaning through concrete details.

Start by asking: Where in my poem am I telling instead of showing? Are there moments where I say "I felt sad" or "It was beautiful" without giving a picture that helps the reader feel or see what I mean? Telling statements can be useful in a first draft, but in revision, you want to replace them with sensory detail and metaphor that reveal that emotion more powerfully.

Let's look at an example.

First Draft:

I walked through the garden
I felt the dew on my toes.
Oh where was I stepping?
Only me and the mouse knows.

This poem tells us what the speaker is feeling, but it doesn't

let us feel it with them. Let's revise by focusing on imagery.
Revised Version:

Tiptoeing through the dew laden garden,
It cooled and soothed my soul
But oh! Where was I stepping?
Only me and the bruised mouse know.

Now we feel what the speaker is going through. "Cooled and soothed" creates a sense of peace before the turn. "Bruised mouse" makes the action that happened much clearer and funnier.. These images are more vivid, emotional, and memorable.

During revision, pay attention to *what kind* of images you're using. Are they fresh, or are they overused? Phrases like "a heart of stone" or "cold as ice" might be true, but they've been said a thousand times. Try to find images that only *you* would think of.

Ask yourself: What do I see in this moment? What do I hear? What's the smallest detail I noticed that others might overlook? Often, the strongest imagery comes from zooming in.

One useful strategy is to highlight every sentence or line in your poem that simply "tells" something. Try rewriting it using at least one sense. Turn "I was angry" into "My hands curled into fists so tight my nails left marks." Turn "The sky was beautiful" into "Lavender clouds melted over the treetops."

To sum up: This week's revision work is about helping your poem show, not tell. Use fresh, specific imagery to create emotion, atmosphere, and meaning. Let your reader feel what you felt by building the scene around them.

When a poem is full of strong images, it becomes unforgettable—not because it told the reader what to feel, but because it *made them feel it.*

Lesson 10 Activity

Purpose of the Activity:
This activity encourages students to revisit a previously written poem and sharpen its imagery through focused revision. By identifying flat or abstract lines and replacing them with sensory details or figurative language, students develop the ability to revise with purpose.

Guided Learning:
1. **Choose a poem to revise.**
   Students select one or more poems from Lesson 9. Encourage them to pick one that feels meaningful but may still have lines that are too vague or abstract.
2. **Identify the core image or emotion.**
   Ask students to write a one-sentence summary of what they want the reader to feel, picture, or understand after reading their poem. This helps focus the revision process.
3. **Highlight lines to improve.**
   Students read their poem and look for any linking verbs or generic five sense word ("I felt..")
4. **Rewrite those lines with imagery.**
   For each underlined line, students write a new sensory image, comparison, or word picture.
5. **Optional peer review.**
   Students may exchange poems with a partner and ask:
   - Which image stands out the most?
   - Is there a moment you wanted to see more clearly?
   - Do any lines still feel too general or "told" instead of shown?

Scoring Options:
Traditional Grading: Use the "Poem Revision" Rubric found in Appendix A. Review their poem revisions as a group on one rubric. This activity is worth 25 points.
Benchmark Grading: This activity is worth 25 points. Award all the

points if they reflect on and revise at least one poem.

Choose one, two, or three of the poems from this unit to revise. Are you telling the reader how you feel—or showing them through a picture? Can the reader *see* the emotion, or just hear about it?

Go through your poem and highlight any linking verb (was, is, has, be) or any sense word (smell, feel, taste, look).

Then replace those areas with an image. Look for opportunities to add:
- **Concrete sensory details** (What did it sound like? What did it feel like?)
- **Unexpected comparisons** (similes or metaphors)
- **Symbolic or emotional objects** (a foggy mirror, a broken shoelace, a flickering lamp)

Optional: The revision process works best with a partner–a parent, sibling, or friend. Have them read your poem and ask them:
- What are some ways that I can add more sensory details?
- What images could replace abstract ideas?

Bonus Revision Lesson: Final Poems Activity

Objective:
Students will revisit their full body of work from the course, choosing selected poems for deeper revision and reflecting on their personal growth as a writer. They will apply multiple tools learned across all five units and generate new material using previously discarded lines and images.

Overview:
This final lesson encourages students to take ownership of their writing process and reflect on their development as poets. Not every poem will be a masterpiece—and that's part of the journey. Through a second round of revision, students will revisit earlier work with fresh eyes, applying tools they didn't yet know when they first wrote the piece. They'll also mine "discarded" poems for powerful lines and phrases, using them to generate new poems or experimental pieces. This is where students move from following instructions to finding their own voice.

Content Review:
Before beginning, review the major tools covered in each unit:
- **Unit 1:** Poetic purpose
- **Unit 2:** Line breaks, stanza structure
- **Unit 3:** Sound devices (alliteration, repetition, rhyme, rhythm)
- **Unit 4:** Word choice and tone
- **Unit 5:** Imagery and sensory detail

Ask students:
- Which tools do you now use without even thinking?
- Is there a poem you wrote early on that might benefit from something you've only just learned?

Teaching Notes:
- **Normalize "failure."** Let students know that disliking a poem is not a failure—it's part of learning what works and what doesn't. The ability to reflect and revise is the mark of a real writer.
- **Encourage self-curation.** Let students pick which poems are worth saving, which to revise, and which to leave behind. This process mirrors the real editorial choices poets make all the time.
- **Showcase transformation.** Invite students to compare a poem's original draft, first revision, and final version. Highlight even small changes that improve tone, pacing, or clarity.
- **Celebrate voice.** Encourage students to reflect on their growth and celebrate lines they're proud of—even if they don't love the whole poem. Those pieces may become the seeds of something stronger later.
- **Offer freedom.** Remind students that this is their opportunity to break out of the structure of earlier assignments. They can remix, remove, or reinvent anything. The only rule is: **Make it more you.**

Scoring Options:

Traditional Grading:
For Step 1: Give 10 points for selecting sentences.
For Step 2: Use the "Poem Revision" Rubric found in Appendix A. Review their poem revisions as a group on one rubric. This activity is worth 25 points.
For Step 3: Use the "Poem First Draft" Rubric found in Appendix A. In the tools section, you can reference all the tools students learned. This poem is worth 20 points.

Benchmark Grading:

For Step 1: Give 10 points for selecting sentences.
For Step 2: This activity is worth 25 points. Award all the points if they reflect on and revise at least one poem.
For Step 3: This poem is worth 20 points. Award 20 points for completing the poem.

We are going to go back through all your poems and do a SECOND revision on some of them based on what you have learned through these five units. Plus, you will have the opportunity to create some additional poems!

Not all of your poems will require a second revision. But follow these tips as you look over everything you wrote:

- If you simply hate a poem and know that it goes in your personal trash-heap, that's fine–you tried something and it didn't work. You still learned something about the kind of poet you are!
- Before you pitch a poem completely, mine it for the good stuff. Maybe you hate the poem as a whole, but you like that one line or phrase. Save them! We will do that below.
- Use tools across assignments. For example, you didn't learn about Imagery when you wrote your Kitchen Poem. Knowing what you do now, are there any sensory details that you could add? What about sound quality to your One-Sentence Poem?
- You ARE allowed to break any rules of the assignments here. Maybe you wrote your Line-by-line Poem following the instructions, but you actually hate lines 3 and 7. Cut them completely, or write them the way you want to! These are YOUR poems intended to express who YOU are.

Step 1: Gather up the good stuff!!
Read all your poems. Which ones do you want to revise? Set

those aside and DON'T use them here. Look at all your "garbage" poems–the ones you don't like. Use this space and pull out all the good stuff.

Write all the lines or phrases you like in the poems you DON'T want to revise. They don't need to make sense. This is your page of ideas for future poems that you will like!!

Step 2: Revise a Second Time

Now, look at the poems you set aside and revise them a second time.

Pay attention to the tools you didn't know the first time you revised. Add in images, change your word choice, mess with your line breaks, or use any other tool you like!

Step 3 (Optional): Write something new

Use this space to write additional poems.

Suggested idea: Use the lines from Step 1 and create a new idea. You can even create your own "Frankenstein Poem" by putting all your discarded ideas together and see what kind of poem results–move the lines around or change the way they break and make something completely new! You may have to add words or change tenses to make it work. A great example of this can be found in Lesson 8.

Appendix A: Scoring Rubrics

Poem First Draft Scoring Rubric

Use this rubric to score the first draft of each poetry activity. Assign a score from each category based on how well the poem meets the listed expectations. Use the guidelines provided to choose a score range and justify your evaluation with comments if needed.

Criteria	Strong (4-5 points)	Developing (2-3 points)	Needs Work (1 point)
Use of Poetic Tools	Clearly uses at least one poetic tool learned in this or previous lessons with purpose and creativity	Attempts a poetic tool, but use may be unclear or inconsistent	Little or no evidence of poetic tools being used
Originality & Voice	Shows a strong personal voice or a creative approach; feels expressive and unique	Voice is emerging; some original choices or lines stand out	Poem feels flat or generic; writer's voice not yet present
Specificity & Detail	Uses strong, specific language or images that help the reader see, hear, or feel the poem	Some specific language used, but parts remain vague or general	Lacks detail; relies heavily on general or overused phrases
Completion & Effort	Fully completes the activity with care and attention to requirements	Activity completed, but may feel rushed or underdeveloped;	Activity incomplete or shows minimal effort

Scoring Guidance

1. Read the poem once for overall understanding.
2. Re-read while referencing the rubric and assignment to evaluate each category.
3. Assign a number within the range for each category:
    - 4-5: Fully meets or exceeds expectations
    - 2-3: Partial completion or inconsistent development
    - 1: Major gaps or missing content
4. Tally the points from each section for a total score out of 20.

Revision Scoring Rubric

Use this rubric to score the revisions of each unit of poems. Not all poems are required to be revised, so use this rubric to score revisions as a group of poems in each unit. Assign a score from each category based on how well the poem meets the listed expectations. Use the guidelines provided to choose a score range and justify your evaluation with comments if needed.

Note: not all poems need a lot of revision–some might only need minor tweaks or word choice changes. The grade here should reflect the focus and effort made in the changes, not the overall quantity of changes. If the student should have revised a poem but chose not to, utilize the "revision effort" to reflect this.

Criteria	Strong (4-5 points)	Developing (2-3 points)	Needs Work (1 point)
Revision Effort	Clearly revised with care; noticeable changes that improve meaning, sound, or structure	Some revision made; changes are surface-level or incomplete	Minimal or no revision; draft remains mostly unchanged or a poem recommended for revision not included here.
Tool Application	Uses at least one poetic tool more effectively after revision	Some attempt to revise with poetic tools, but usage is still unclear or inconsistent	Poetic tools are unchanged or misused in revision
Clarity & Focus	Revision helps clarify the poem's meaning, emotion, or theme	Poem is somewhat clearer; revision helps in places but may add confusion elsewhere	Poem remains unclear or confusing; revision did not improve understanding
Language & Imagery	Stronger, more vivid word choices or images appear in the revised version	Some improvements in word choice or imagery	Language and imagery are unchanged or still vague
Reflection & Intent	Shows clear understanding of why changes were made; student can explain their choices	Some explanation or evidence of intentional change	Little reflection or awareness of revision goals

Scoring Guidance
1. Review both the first draft of the poem and the revision for each poem included in the unit group (not all poems are required to be revised
2. Assign a number within the range for each category:
   - 4-5: Fully meets or exceeds expectations
   - 2-3: Partial completion or inconsistent development
   - 1: Major gaps or missing content
3. Tally the points from each section for a total score out of 25.

Appendix B: Grade Tracking

Grade Tracking Table – Traditional Grading

Lesson Activity	Activity	Points Earned	Points Possible	Grade
Lesson 1	Kitchen Poem		20	
Lesson 1	Picture/Object Poem		20	
Lesson 1	Persona Confession Poem		20	
Lesson 2	Revise Lesson 1 Poems		25	
Lesson 3	Line Break Poem		20	
Lesson 3	One-Sentence Poem		20	
Lesson 3	Line-Builder Poem		20	
Lesson 4	Revise Lesson 3 Poems		25	
Lesson 5	Random Words, Deliberate Sounds Poem		20	
Lesson 5	Nonsense Poem		20	
Lesson 5	Popping Popcorn Poem		20	
Lesson 6	Revise Lesson 5 Poems		25	
Lesson 7	Line-by-Line Poem		20	
Lesson 7	Nouns & Verbs Poem		20	
Lesson 7	Tone Shift Poem		20	

Lesson 8	Revise Lesson 7 Poems		25	
Lesson 9	Afterimages Poem		20	
Lesson 9	Postcard Poem		20	
Lesson 9	What the Object Knows Poem		20	
Lesson 10	Revise Lesson 9 Poems		25	
Bonus Lesson	Select lines (Step 1)		5	
Bonus Lesson	Revise All Poems		50	
Bonus Lesson	Frankenstein Poem		20	
	TOTAL		**500**	

Grade Tracking Table – Benchmark Grading

Lesson Activity	Activity	Points Earned	Points Possible	Grade	Comments
Lesson 1	Kitchen Poem		20		
Lesson 1	Picture/Object Poem		20		
Lesson 1	Persona Confession Poem		20		
Lesson 2	Revise Lesson 1 Poems		25		
Lesson 3	Line Break Poem		20		
Lesson 3	One-Sentence Poem		20		
Lesson 3	Line-Builder Poem		20		
Lesson 4	Revise Lesson 3 Poems		25		
Lesson 5	Random Words, Deliberate Sounds Poem		20		
Lesson 5	Nonsense Poem		20		
Lesson 5	Popping Popcorn Poem		20		
Lesson 6	Revise Lesson 5 Poems		25		
Lesson 7	Line-by-Line Poem		20		
Lesson 7	Nouns & Verbs Poem		20		
Lesson 7	Tone Shift Poem		20		
Lesson 8	Revise Lesson 7 Poems		25		

Lesson 9	Afterimages Poem		20		
Lesson 9	Postcard Poem		20		
Lesson 9	What the Object Knows Poem		20		
Lesson 10	Revise Lesson 9 Poems		25		
Bonus Lesson	Select lines (Step 1)		5		
Bonus Lesson	Revise All Poems		50		
Bonus Lesson	Frankenstein Poem		20		
	TOTAL		**500**		

Grade Tracking Table – Pass/Fail Grading

Lesson Activity	Activity	Pass/Fail	Comments
Lesson 1	Kitchen Poem		
Lesson 1	Picture/Object Poem		
Lesson 1	Persona Confession Poem		
Lesson 2	Revise Lesson 1 Poems		
Lesson 3	Line Break Poem		
Lesson 3	One-Sentence Poem		
Lesson 3	Line-Builder Poem		
Lesson 4	Revise Lesson 3 Poems		
Lesson 5	Random Words, Deliberate Sounds Poem		
Lesson 5	Nonsense Poem		
Lesson 5	Popping Popcorn Poem		
Lesson 6	Revise Lesson 5 Poems		
Lesson 7	Line-by-Line Poem		
Lesson 7	Nouns & Verbs Poem		
Lesson 7	Tone Shift Poem		
Lesson 8	Revise Lesson 7 Poems		
Lesson 9	Afterimages Poem		

Lesson 9	Postcard Poem		
Lesson 9	What the Object Knows Poem		
Lesson 10	Revise Lesson 9 Poems		
Bonus Lesson	Select lines (Step 1)		
Bonus Lesson	Revise All Poems		
Bonus Lesson	Frankenstein Poem		
	OVERALL		